WALL STREET
AND REGULATION

WALL STREET
AND REGULATION

edited by Samuel L. Hayes, III

HBS
PRESS

Harvard Business School Press

Boston, Massachusetts

HARVARD BUSINESS SCHOOL PRESS

Library of Congress Cataloging-in-Publication Data

Wall Street and regulation.

   Includes bibliographies and index.
   1. Banking law—United States.   2. Investments—
Law and legislation—United States.   I. Hayes, Samuel L.
KF974.W35   1987   346.73'092   87-8654
ISBN 0-87584-183-X (alk. paper) 347.30692

        90 89 88 87   5 4 3 2 1

Contents

Acknowledgments

The production of *Wall Street and Regulation* has mobilized the energies of a number of people. The original inspiration was the impending retirement of Charles M. Williams from the Harvard Business School faculty, and it was in celebration of his distinguished career that so many other people enthusiastically devoted their time to the staging of the Research Colloquium on Changes in the U.S. Financial Services Sector in June 1986. Professor E. Raymond Corey, as chairman of the Division of Research at the School, gave enormous encouragement and support, as did a host of other colleagues, including George Hollenbeck who served as administrator for the Colloquium. Session leaders played a key role in focusing discussion and testing ideas contained in the research papers and we are therefore grateful to the leadership of M. Colyer Crum, Charles M. Williams, Dwight B. Crane, Robert G. Eccles, Jr., W. Carl Kester, Jay W. Lorsch, George G. C. Parker, and Henry W. Reiling. We are, of course, indebted to the sixty-five Colloquium participants representing various dimensions of the U.S. financial services sector, government, and academia. Their comments and suggestions on the papers were important in shaping the final versions that appear here.

To produce a book focused primarily on aspects of financial services regulations, it was necessary to omit several important Colloquium papers with broader topics. We are, nonetheless, grateful to Frederick G. Fisher III, Linda A. Hill, Jeffrey A. Sonnenfeld, and Philip A. Wellons for their excellent research studies which so enriched the Colloquium sessions.

John M. Case did invaluable research for us and the editorial assistance of Earl Harbert and Andrew Kopecki is also gratefully acknowledged. Ms Duncan Bauer and Ms Helen Pakstis transcribed numerous versions of the papers and were patient and long-suffering.

Boston, Massachusetts   Samuel L. Hayes, III
January 1987

For Charles M. Williams

George Gund Professor of
Commercial Banking
Emeritus

In honor of his distinguished career
as teacher and scholar at the
Harvard Business School

WALL STREET
AND REGULATION

ONE

INTRODUCTION

The U.S. financial services sector has probably undergone more structural change in the past decade than during all of the period since the Great Depression of the 1930s. This is a development of worldwide importance, given the global position of the United States in the post–World War II world and the fact that numerous countries have sought to emulate one or more features of the U.S. banking and financial services sector. The mid-1980s thus presents a particularly timely point to examine some key developments in the U.S. financial markets and the regulatory mechanisms that monitor and control them.

The co-authors of this volume were particularly interested in exploring how the philosophy of regulatory oversight has evolved in the context of competitive patterns unfolding in the financial services sector. How has it worked in practice? Which dimensions of these historical regulatory arrangements have obsolesced? Which have been enduring? What dimensions of financial competition are most (or least) responsive to regulatory remedies? The writers share a belief that the contemporary U.S. financial and regulatory mosaic is not a spontaneous ordering of the moment but, rather, the product of a complex historical evolution. And although the United States is a relatively young country, the existing pattern of financial services is nonetheless influenced by economic and political events, as well as regulatory attitudes, that trace back to the earliest days of the republic. This is amply demonstrated by the comprehensive review of the unfolding regulatory climate in the U.S. financial services sector presented in chapter two and by chapter three's examination of the political, regulatory, and economic currents that have directed the U.S. commercial banking sector over the past 150 years.

The decade of the 1930s stands out as a watershed in terms of organizational structure and regulatory climate within the U.S. financial services sector. The implicit political compact between the private-sector financial community, on the one hand, and governmental units representing the public interest, on the other, had broken down. There was a perception that the coun-

1

try had been abused by a rapacious banking fraternity, and this set the stage for important structural change in the financial services sector. The election of a populist president and Congress in 1932 carried with it a mandate to take strong measures to "do something" to correct these perceived abuses.

Chapters two, three, and five discuss various dimensions of those reforms, which were far-reaching and relatively radical in the context of the existing arrangements in other western industrialized countries. But the new political leadership in Washington took bold steps to restore public confidence in the capitalistic system because it perceived the system to be under increasing attack, particularly in light of the Marxist regime that had recently taken power in Russia.

The enactment of these reforms was followed soon after by the disruption of World War II; thus a period of some ten years of extraordinary circumstances ensued that permitted no real test of the viability of the new rules. Following World War II, however, there was a long period during which the United States experienced a new equilibrium in its financial services sector; the financing environment was relatively uncomplicated and the regulatory machinery set in place during the 1930s appeared to serve quite well. The credit alternatives available to individual and commercial borrowers were comparatively few and straightforward. Short-term working capital needs were routinely handled by bank lines of credit. Much of the intermediate-term financing was obtained via term loans from a bank, and long-term capital was raised via a private placement with an insurance company. If the borrower was of sufficient size and credit stature, it could utilize a public bond offering underwritten by an investment banker with whom the issuer usually had an established relationship. The rules for such issuances were explicitly laid down and carefully followed by the designated financing intermediaries, particularly with regard to "due diligence" investigative requirements (rules designed to ensure that full information relevant to the issuer's affairs were in the hands of investors at the time of the sale).

At the outset of the postwar period, institutional money provided considerable debt funds, but individuals were still the most important suppliers of equity capital. And while individual investors had been much buffeted and battered by the stock market crash and subsequent economic depression, they nonetheless continued to follow predictable savings habits in the postwar period that assured a stable source of funds for commercial and savings banks and for the investment banking underwriters who guaranteed to issuers the ultimate placement of their newly offered securities at agreed-upon prices.

With real economic growth in the United States averaging 3.2 percent annually during the fifteen-year period from 1946 to 1960, the banking intermediaries who provided the financing support for this robust level of private-sector activity earned sizable revenues. Thus, although the reform legislation of the 1930s had divided up the financing terrain in what some thought was an arbitrary manner, the major financial intermediaries largely acceded to the legislation; it appeared to offer both an umbrella of protection against the well-remembered wrath of the public after the profligate 1920s and an effective barrier to unwelcome competition. With each group's designated business territory in the financing landscape growing comfortably, there was little incentive to encroach on the territory of other financial intermediaries and thereby to disturb the unspoken pax "financus" that appeared to be serving everyone reasonably well.

Meanwhile, the institutionalization of savings was under way, as chronicled in chapter four and elsewhere in this book. This long-range trend, which really began in the wake of the reform legislation of the 1930s, had grown important enough by the 1960s to spawn new investment firms—including Salomon Brothers and Donaldson, Lufkin & Jenrette—that were geared exclusively to servicing the special requirements of this much enhanced institutional investor constituency. As pension funds and other pools of individuals' savings grew progressively larger, their influence on the financial markets and on the financing strategies of capital users also grew.

This book documents the increasing strain caused by the maintenance of the status quo in the financial services area as the postwar U.S. economic surge faltered and ultimately stalled. Growth in GNP slowed during the 1960s and into the 1970s, and this slowdown was accompanied by a secular increase in the rate of inflation. The primary and secondary effects of this accelerating inflation fundamentally altered the long-established savings patterns of individuals who, as chapter three makes clear, increasingly eschewed traditional investment vehicles in favor of newer, more market-sensitive instruments such as money market funds.

Inflation also had a major impact on capital users and large institutional investors. Corporate capital users shopped for funds with an increasingly sharp pencil, and as chapter three documents, they awarded business to intermediaries who provided them with specialized financing instruments mathematically designed to optimize the issuer's risk-reward trade-offs. The advent of economic disruptions in the 1970s, such as the higher cost of money and the floating of exchange rates, spurred major capital users to expand further their internal financial capabilities to the point where many of the formerly value-added services provided by outside vendors were now either completely internalized or reduced to commodity status and awarded largely on a price basis. This had the effect of eroding the corporate issuers' long-standing and stable relationships not only with their commercial banks but also with their investment banks. The growth of competitively placed "shelf" underwritings (securities issues pre-registered for rapid sale when a window of market opportunity opened), discussed in chapter six, is a prime example of the fragmenting of relationships in the securities sector.

Chapter four discusses the growing size and increasing sophistication of institutional investors, particularly the private-sector corporate pension funds. This has led to a continuing evolution in investment decision making that has brought more and more of the strategic funds management of these pools "in-house" (i.e., under the management of the internal staffs of the sponsoring company or organization).

A number of scholars and regulators have maintained that this increasing sophistication of securities market activity—both in the primary and in the secondary sectors—has had the salutary effect of making markets more reflective of the true underlying value of those securities; that is, it has made the markets more "efficient." Certainly the complex investment hedging and arbitraging schemes (epitomized by "program trading," detailed in chapter four) would seem to point in that direction. In addition, it was partly on this presumption of market efficiency that the Securities and Exchange Commission launched the experiment with shelf registrations (chronicled in chapter six). Both program trading and shelf registrations have had other effects that make some observers uneasy: program trading has increased the short-term volatility of the markets even as it purportedly works to make them more efficient; and shelf registrations are typically sold on such short notice that there is not enough time to undertake the prudent investigation of the issuer's affairs.

Looming in the background throughout this book is the growing influence of the offshore financial markets. An important part of the impetus for initiating shelf registrations in the United States, for instance, has been attributed to the increasingly attractive alternative of floating bonds in the Euromarkets—a realistic alternative for a growing number of U.S. private-sector companies as well as a number of U.S. municipalities that seek taxable financings as a consequence of changes in the 1986 Tax Act.

Among the most important implications of this myriad of recent competitive and regulatory changes in the U.S. financial markets is the status of the social compact between the financial services industry and the public mentioned earlier; it was, after all, the system's perceived abuses of the public that precipitated the regulatory reforms of the 1930s, and these, in turn, have shaped the industry's evolution during the last half-century. A priceless quote (in chapter six) attributed to Henry O. Havemeyer, then president of American Sugar Refining Company, captures eloquently the contempt that the public felt was emanating from Wall Street insiders:

> Let the buyer beware; that covers the whole business. You cannot wet-nurse people from the time they are born until the day they die. They have to wade in and get stuck and that is the way men are educated and cultivated.

Chapter six provocatively explores whether the post–1930s' regulation that supplanted the earlier benign neglect has accrued any net economic or "fairness" benefits to investors.

The concluding chapter draws together some of the major competitive and regulatory insights of the preceding chapters and suggests possible directions for the future.

TWO

REGULATION-DEFINED FINANCIAL MARKETS: FRAGMENTATION AND INTEGRATION IN FINANCIAL SERVICES

Richard H. K. Vietor

For half a century now, government has played an immense role in American financial markets, as lender, borrower, intermediary, and regulator.[1] But the government's role as regulator—the controller of price, product, and industry structure—increasingly appears to have been an anomaly, a temporary departure from competitive and integrated markets. Of course, the same might be said for regulation of airlines, trucking and rail transportation, telecommunications, and natural gas. But none of these types of regulation can claim as long a pedigree.

Until the Great Depression, financial markets in America were relatively free. Diversified merchant banks competed for corporate clients, while several thousand unit banks provided local financial services under state supervision. When this system collapsed (or at least failed to serve the public interest), federal legislators imposed controls that segmented markets and atomized industry structure; these controls eventually metastasized into an elaborate regulatory regime that shaped almost every aspect of financial management.

With the prosperity of the 1950s and 1960s these regulation-defined financial markets expanded rapidly. Overlapping regulatory authorities supervised, shaped, and protected the various types of specialized financial intermediaries: commercial banks, thrifts, securities firms, insurance companies, and investment funds. The growth and development of these industries was accompanied by a parallel evolution of political and professional institutions such as trade associations, professional groups, congressional committees, and regulatory bureaucracies with vested interests in the system.

When in the early 1970s basic economic conditions began to change, this elaborate regulatory system did not immediately adjust; its political and institutional inertia was overwhelming. But as the gap widened between regulation and market reality, it created distortions of price, supply, and demand. Intense competitive pressures, in the form of disintermediation and the circumvention of regulatory product-market barriers, ensued. As these pressures accumulated over several years and destabilized the financial system, they gave rise to the new political alliances necessary to change public policy.[2]

This chapter has two objectives. First, it describes the framework of regulation that has defined American financial markets and institutions for the past fifty years. The analysis will focus on federal regulation of price, product, scope of market, and industry structure. Other important aspects of regulation, such as monetary policy, securities issuance, actuarial procedures, and the operational standards that govern bank chartering, examination, liquidity, consumer protection, and disclosure, will receive only cursory attention. The second objective is to provide perspective on the dynamic relationship between government and business in the financial services industry. In no other industry has government played a greater role or has change been so evident in times of crisis. Managers in this industry must function in two competitive arenas—one economic, the other political. The evolving interaction of these two environments not only affects operations; in a more significant way, it also affects strategy.

FREE BANKING AND INTEGRATED FINANCE (1837–1933)

The era of free banking commenced in 1837, when the charter of the Second Bank of the United States expired, and it ended in 1933, when Congress passed the Banking Act (also known as the Glass-Steagall Act); both dates mark times of national controversy over corporate power, monopoly, and special privilege.

The label "free banking" is something of a misnomer, for it suggests an absence of regulation. But during this period of nearly one hundred years, state governments did regulate state-chartered banks in matters of safety and soundness. With the National Banking Acts of 1863 and 1864, however, the federal government, through the Office of the Comptroller of the Currency, also got involved in the regulation of nationally chartered banks. Yet this dual supervisory system was not designed to eliminate competition; instead, the critical factor in both was free entry. Here the State of New York led the way with its Free Banking Act of 1838, which set minimal terms for chartering. As other states followed New York's lead, the number of state-chartered banks jumped from 713 in 1838 to 1,466 by 1863.[3] Prices (interest rates) were effectively set by supply and demand (although usury laws fixed ceilings on loan-interest rates), product portfolios were largely discretionary (although invariably under attack), and industry structure, with the important exception of branching, remained unrestrained.

Basically, the National Banking Act of 1863 was an attempt to create institutional buyers for government securities that were issued to finance the Civil War. Its terms authorized nationally chartered banks to issue notes, backed by Treasury bonds; it also imposed a tax on the notes of state-chartered banks. With these incentives, more than a thousand state banks switched charters during the next few years. For these national banks, the act set reserve requirements, prohibited stock trading, and created a Comptroller of the Currency to supervise chartering and perform examinations. Since they operated under fewer restrictions, state-chartered banks continued to attract new entrants by devising such innovations as the demand deposit.[4]

One of the Comptroller's first rulings (in 1864) restricted branch banking by nationally chartered banks. In the mid-nineteenth century, this rule made little difference; most states maintained a similar prohibition, urban areas were small, and electronic communications between offices did not yet exist. But by 1900, this rule had become restrictive. Since several states had allowed limited branching in metropolitan areas, state-chartered banks enjoyed an advantage over national banks. In effect, the Comptroller's ban constrained the growth of national banks, distorted their natural structure, and caused more defections from national banking.[5]

Under these conditions, the number and variety of deposit-taking institutions increased rapidly. Since commercial and private bankers initially focused on wholesale corporate finance, there were attractive opportunities for mutual banks, savings and loan associations (S&Ls), and, eventually, credit unions to

serve niches in the retail financial markets for small-business
owners, farmers, urban wage-earners, and residential mortgage
holders. By World War I, more than 25,000 commercial banks,
6,000 S&Ls, and 600 mutual savings banks were operating in
the United States.[6] During the same period, private (investment) banks, insurance companies, and trust companies were
left free to grow and compete.

By the turn of the century, about 250 unincorporated investment banking houses, located primarily in New York, Boston,
and Philadelphia, had come to dominate the business of underwriting, distributing, and brokering corporate issues of long-term
debt and equity. The most prominent of these firms, such as
Morgan, Kidder Peabody, Kuhn Loeb, and Halsley Stuart, had
grown prosperous during the second half of the nineteenth century by serving the financial needs of railroads, utilities, state
and local governments, foreign governments, international traders, and (eventually) industrial manufacturers. Until the early
1900s investment banking remained a wholesale business, based
on close, private relationships between bankers and their
clients.[7] But with the emergence of individual investors, large
securities flotations, and trading in secondary markets, private
investment banking became a matter of larger public interest.[8]

The life and property-liability insurance industries grew rapidly and haphazardly during the nineteenth century, with little
regulation. After the 1850s, several progressive states created
insurance commissioners to license and supervise (at least min-
imally) industry practices. A system of independent agents developed, and the intense price competition that emerged perhaps contributed to the instability and frequent insolvencies
that characterized the insurance industry. Organized pricing cartels also appeared (and usually failed); they were eventually out-
lawed in twenty states.[9] Overall, this combination of unrestricted growth, frequent failures, price fixing, and unethical
practices fueled public dissatisfaction with the insurance industry and captured the attention of Progressive "muckrakers."[10]

At the same time, trust companies, such as Guaranty, Bankers Trust, and some three hundred other firms combined the
functions of commercial banking, investment banking, insurance, and more; they managed estates, cared for property, and
made investments. "These wide powers," noted one observer,

"attract customers." By 1900, trust companies (organized under general incorporation laws) controlled about $1 billion in deposits—equal to the sum held by state-chartered commercial banks and two-fifths of the deposits of national banks.[11] Their ability to provide this "department-store" style of financial service, without any regulation, resulted in a fivefold increase in the number of such firms by 1910.[12]

By the turn of the century, privately owned firms in the financial services sector controlled very large capital holdings and competed intensely in a relatively unrestricted environment. With other peoples' money at stake, however, political scrutiny and legislative intervention seemed inevitable. Investigation and regulation became the order of the day; reform was in the air.

Insurance reform came first. In New York during the summer of 1905, the Armstrong investigation revealed serious improprieties, mismanagement, and influence peddling in the life insurance industry. Charles Evans Hughes drew national attention, as he interrogated and then shamed industry leaders. New York and several other states responded with legislation that gave insurance commissioners additional responsibilities.[13] Another New York legislative investigation a few years later (this one by the Merritt committee), focused on the problems of fire insurance. As a result, in 1911 New York enacted a law to permit "action in concert in the fixing of fire insurance rates." Ironically, this measure appeared to protect insurance companies from excess competition, rather than protect consumers from excess costs.[14]

In banking, the Comptroller did sound an alarm in 1902.[15] Concerned by the increasing involvement of national banks in securities sales, he ruled that corporate bonds must be limited to 10 percent of a bank's capital.[16] In 1907, after a severe financial panic had rocked the American economy, a national monetary commission recommended creation of a central bank to manage the currency and maintain liquidity. Public pressure for reform intensified in 1912 as a result of the Pujo committee's revelations about the "money trust." This House Banking Committee investigation (under Rep. Pujo) examined financial power and interlocking directorships among investment bankers.[17] Representative Pujo's committee found that commercial banks such as

National City Bank and the First National Bank of New York were risking conflict of interest by underwriting and selling corporate securities; its report urged that banks be prohibited from dealing in securities.[18]

As an acknowledgment of the problem in banking, Congress passed the Federal Reserve Act in 1913. The act established twelve regional reserve banks and a governing board in Washington and required all nationally chartered banks to become members. State-chartered banks and trusts could also join the system, without giving up their affiliated securities activities. The reserve banks were authorized to rediscount short-term commercial and agricultural paper for member banks and later given power to provide various transaction services. The Federal Reserve Board originally consisted of five presidential appointees plus the Comptroller and the Secretary of the Treasury; it was responsible for setting reserve requirements and maintaining liquidity in the banking system.[19]

These midcourse corrections did nothing to restrain the expansion of financial markets, and World War I accelerated the pace of growth by creating a vast new pool of government securities and by stimulating personal savings and expanding the market for corporate equities. The total number of commercial banks (and branches) increased rapidly until 1922, but it fell thereafter as a result of consolidations and suspensions; the number of S&Ls exceeded 12,000, there were over 1,500 trust companies, and life insurance companies numbered more than 400. Table 2-1 shows the dramatic asset growth for selected financial institutions; the growth for all depository institutions was nearly threefold, and for insurance companies it was even more.[20]

During the 1920s, in the securities sector the volume of bond issues more than doubled to almost $65 billion.[21] The number of issues listed on the New York Stock Exchange rose to 1,278 (from 136 in 1865), while several thousand independent brokers and dealers participated in a booming over-the-counter market. The portion of personal wealth in the form of securities reached 75 percent by 1932 (from 23 percent in 1908).

This burst of growth in the securities markets, combined with the intense competition among financial services vendors, brought forth increased innovation and integration. Commercial banks expanded by branching and by forming securities

Table 2-1
Asset Growth of Financial Institutions, 1913–1930
($ billions)

Date	National Banks		State Banks		Mutual Savings Banks		Loan & Trust Companies		Building and Loan Assns.	
	No.	Assets	No.	Assets	No.	Assets	No.	Assets	No.	Assets
1913	7,473	$11.04	14,011	$ 4.14	1,978	$ 5.23	1,515	$ 5.12	—	n.a.
1922	8,246	20.93	18,232	13.06	1,685	7.93	1,550	8.53	9,255	$2.89
1927	7,536	26.58	15,690	16.56	1,461	10.82	1,647	13.99	—	n.a.
1930	7,252	29.12	13,582	15.27	1,320	11.81	1,564	17.70	11,777	$8.83

Source: Office of the Comptroller of the Currency, *Annual Report*, 1913, 1922, 1931.

affiliates; investment trusts syndicated shares in the huge new debt market; and securities brokers increasingly accommodated their customers' frenzied demands by selling stock on margin.

Prior to World War I, branching by state-chartered banks had generally been encouraged as a means of getting bank services out to local markets. Under a 1918 statute designed to deter defections from the Federal Reserve System, even national banks had also been allowed to acquire branch systems.[22] And in 1922, the Comptroller ruled that "tellers' windows" (limited-service branches) were permissible for national banks. But thereafter, as the number of banks declined from its peak of 30,000, local political resistance to branching stiffened. Two years later, moreover, the Supreme Court upheld the states' authority to prevent branching by national banks.[23]

Between 1924 and 1927, the issue of branch banking was extensively debated in the banking industry, in state governments, and in Congress. The result, a compromise of sorts, was the McFadden Act of 1927. According to Representative McFadden, this bill was designed to slow defections from the national banking system. On the one hand, the measure put national banks on an equal footing with state banks, and where state laws allowed, intracity branching was opened to all. On the other hand, the McFadden Act curtailed any new branching outside the city of a bank's headoffice. State banks benefited disproportionately from this provision, since their existing networks of intercity branches were grandfathered. The act, as McFadden candidly acknowledged, was "an antibranch banking bill."[24]

Alongside efforts to expand geographically, banks attempted to expand their product lines into securities. The First Securities Company, incorporated in 1908 by the First National Bank of New York, was the first important securities affiliate of a commercial bank. But commercial bankers did not fully realize either the market's potential or their own competitive advantage in bundling financial services until after their wartime experience handling treasury bonds. By 1922 sixty-two commercial banks were engaged in investment banking and had opened branches in cities across the country. This proliferation brought forth a blunt warning from the Comptroller that these institutions were dangerous vehicles, vulnerable to scheming and speculation; his warning went unheeded.[25] By 1927, bank affiliates originated 13 percent of new debt issues and participated in another 7 percent.[26]

The McFadden Act, written to prevent defections from national banking, confirmed the legality of securities affiliates (a matter left unclear in Section 5136 of the Federal Reserve Act). Although Senator Carter Glass adamantly opposed it and complained that "there is nothing in the national banking act that permits it," Congress approved the security-affiliate provision with little debate.[27] After passage of the act, "department-store banking" really took off.[28] By 1931, 285 national bank affiliates and numerous state banks were engaged in investment banking. More remarkably, banks increased their share of originations to more than 40 percent, and their participations to 61 percent.[29] During the years 1931 through 1933, the Investment Bankers Association of America elected presidents drawn from the securities affiliates of commercial banks;[30] private investment banks were nearly left in the dust.

Investment trusts were a third (hybrid) innovation; they were slow to emerge, and in 1920 there was only a handful of them. These new organizations issued shares to individual investors and reinvested the funds in a portfolio of securities. Investors in these trusts presumably benefited from the trusts' risk-spreading and expertise. Some of these companies were organized by professional managers and trustees; others, increasingly, were set up by investment banks and by the securities affiliates of commercial banks to take advantage of underwritings and to provide a broader bundle of services to customers. Between 1921 and 1929, more than 700 investment trusts were organized, with total holdings of $7 billion. The rate of growth and the degree of vertical integration (and therefore leverage) were noted by some critics prior to 1929, but nothing was done: "When the crash came," Vincent Carosso wrote, "investment trusts went down with 'a deadening thud.' "[31] The economic freedom of commercial and investment banking went down with them.

REGULATORY STABILIZATION (1933–1945)

By the late winter of 1933, the American financial community had been totally discredited. During nine days of relentless questioning by Ferdinand Pecora, counsel to the Senate Banking

Commitee, one executive after another from the nation's largest
banks and investment houses admitted to practices that ranged
from negligence to outrageousness. These revelations, according
to the *New York Times*, shocked the "moral sense of the
nation."[32]

The Pecora hearings were the last straw; the stock market
crash, the destruction of financial assets, the eight-thousand
bank failures since 1929, and the debilitating recession had already shaken America's faith in free markets. Thousands of
Americans, through no fault of their own, had lost their savings;
competition seemed to be a failure. Excess capacity and excess
competition fueled risk-taking, speculation, self-dealing, and
imprudence by investment bankers, investment trusts, commercial banks, and (to a lesser extent) thrift and life insurance
businesses. The financial community itself was in desperate
straits and was nearly as dissatisfied as the public. To prevent
a total collapse of the banking system, President Franklin
Roosevelt declared a national bank holiday on March 6, 1933.[33]

These failures of substance and confidence resulted in a raft of
legislation: the Federal Home Loan Bank Act of 1932, the
Banking Act of 1933, the Securities Act of 1933, the Securities
Exchange Act of 1934, the Federal Credit Union Act of 1934,
the Banking Act of 1935, the Maloney Act of 1938, the Investment Company Act of 1940, and the McCarran-Ferguson Act of
1945. Each act, by itself, was the product of intense political
contention and maneuvering among diverse banking and securities interests, bureaucracies, and legislative coalitions; taken together, these laws restructured the financial system. They established a maze of new operating standards, segmented asset and
liability markets by type and territory, fixed prices, and established guarantees against risk. Stability was the overriding objective, and governmental control and monopoly markets were the
results.

Nonbank, depository institutions—primarily savings & loan
associations (S&Ls) and mutual savings banks—were the hard-
est hit and the first to respond. The United States Building and
Loan League began intense lobbying in 1931, and by 1932 it had
succeeded in getting Congress to enact a bill, drafted by League
officials, that created the Federal Home Loan Bank Board
(FHLBB). The responsibilities of the FHLBB were similar to

those of the Federal Reserve: it was to provide liquidity to the S&Ls through funds borrowed in the capital markets. Commercial banks, which might have contributed to this bailout of the mortgage market, were excluded.[34] A year later, the FHLBB received authority to charter and supervise federal S&Ls. In 1934, when Congress established the Federal Savings and Loan Insurance Corporation (FSLIC), the FHLBB gained supervisory control over the state-chartered thrifts that applied for federal deposit insurance. A parallel system for federal credit unions was created that same year.

The centerpiece of legislative reform, and thus of national policy, was the Banking Act of 1933 (and its sequel in 1935). This law, often called the Glass-Steagall Act, revised branching restrictions, created federal deposit insurance, imposed interest-rate ceilings on deposits, strengthened the Federal Reserve, and decoupled commercial banking from investment banking. Special interests within the banking community contested each of these changes, and none was passed without controversy.

The drive for banking reform had been initiated several years earlier by Carter Glass, Republican chairman of the Senate Banking Committee's subcommittee to review national banking. Glass, who was one of the original sponsors of the Federal Reserve Act of 1913, was deeply disturbed by the reoccurrence of financial panic. He firmly believed that although the Federal Reserve System was well designed, it had failed to manage monetary policy aggressively. Problems of industry structure and conduct—"unsound affiliations" and "evil practices"—appeared to have caused bank failures and the stock market collapse.[35] In reaching these conclusions, Glass and his subcommittee relied heavily on the advice of H. Parker Willis, a finance professor at Columbia University. Willis generally subscribed to the orthodoxy of the real bills doctrine, which equated real investment with household savings.

The purpose of commercial banking, according to Willis, was short-term lending; thus, any involvement of bank affiliates in bonded debt seemed theoretically unsound. In its early 1931 deliberations, the Glass committee first considered a program that would have severely regulated but still permitted securities affiliates of commercial banks. But committee members received so many letters from citizens who were "outraged" by the injustices of the affiliate system that they finally opted for the complete separation of commercial and investment banking.[36] Later, the Pecora hearings (in 1933) made separation a political necessity; even bankers accepted it as inevitable. Winthrop Aldrich, president of Chase National Bank, summed up the banks' newly found sense of responsibility:

> Many of the abuses in the banking situation had arisen from failure to discern that commercial banking and investment banking are two fields of activity essentially different in nature. . . . The commercial bank's credit function is very definitely governed by its responsibility to meet its deposit liabilities on demand. It must not seek excessive profits by taking undue credit risks, and it cannot wisely tie up its funds in long-term credits however safe they may be.[37]

In its final form, the Banking Act prohibited commercial banks that were members of the Federal Reserve System from underwriting, purchasing, or selling corporate securities on their own account. Banks could not be affiliated with, in any manner, or have interlocking directorships with securities firms or investment trusts. Conversely, securities firms were prohibited from accepting deposits that were subject to withdrawal by checking, passbook, or certificates; liquidation or divestment was required of existing securities affiliates.[38]

With similar logic, the Glass committee felt that the solution to liquidity crises (runs on deposits) lay not in deposit insurance but in an institutional mechanism for managing liquidations more efficiently, in tougher reserve requirements, in greater liquidity, and in liberalization of branching restrictions. Deposit guarantees, according to Willis, were really asset guarantees—something for which government should not be responsible. In the event of the failure of financial institutions, the public interest was best served by the prompt restoration of access to deposits; this, in turn, was best achieved through efficient, institutional reorganizations.[39] During the 1920s, however, public support for deposit insurance had grown with the number of bank failures, and state programs had proved unequal to the task. By 1933, support for federal deposit insurance was overwhelming, especially from mid-western populists in the House of Representatives.

Although big banks adamantly opposed deposit insurance, thousands of smaller, undercapitalized unit banks outside the money centers saw deposit insurance as a preferable alternative to the liberalized branching favored by Senator Glass. Clearly, the controversy over branch banking had not been resolved by the McFadden Act. Smaller, rural banks had successfully prevented intercity branching in most states on the grounds that the "money trust" would destroy competition and drain the countryside of its savings. To skirt these restrictions, "chain" or "group" banks (holding companies that owned multiple banks) had grown rapidly since 1927.

Senator Glass was a leading advocate of liberalized branching as a means of improving the capitalization and liquidity of each bank (office) and of reducing risk by dilution. To prevent drainage of local deposits to money centers, Glass proposed restricting interest rates on interbank demand deposits. Big banks, however, remained unsupportive; intercity branching threatened both their urban bases and their correspondent relationships. The original Glass bill, which proposed statewide branching by national banks (irrespective of state laws), did not even win support from the full committee.[40]

In 1933, Senator Glass was forced to concede defeat on branch banking and, ironically, to lobby hard in favor of deposit insurance. Although President Roosevelt supported banking reform in principle, he declared that both of these specific measures were too radical. The Banking Act that was enacted created a Federal Deposit Insurance Corporation (FDIC), to which all Federal Reserve members had to subscribe. The FDIC fully guaranteed deposits up to $10,000 and guaranteed 75 percent of deposits up to $50,000 and 50 percent of larger deposits. As for branching, the act only stipulated that national banks be fully equal to state banks and thus allowed intercity branching when state law concurred.[41]

The bank holding company, however, already offered an alternate route to geographic expansion. By 1931, 97 group banks (as the holding companies were called) controlled 978 commercial banks. In order to plug this potentially destabilizing loophole, the Banking Act of 1933 authorized the Federal Reserve Board to regulate such companies in terms of examination, reserves, and asset concentration (the 10 percent liquidity rule). In 1935, Congress amended this provision to exempt one-bank holding companies.[42]

The Banking Act also accomplished two other major changes; it prohibited payment of interest on demand deposits and authorized the Federal Reserve Board to regulate interest rates on time deposits (subsequently implemented as Regulation Q). This extraordinary measure, which amounted to the imposition of price controls on the liability side of the balance sheet, created no controversy at the time even though it derived from no apparent economic rationale. Neither the hearings nor previous versions of the bill had considered anything other than a liberal interest-rate ceiling on interbank deposits, and empirical studies conducted since 1933 had not revealed any evidence that competition for deposits had been destructive or unusually intense.[43] Senator Glass claimed, however, that the act was intended "to put a stop to the competition between banks in payment of interest, which frequently induce[s] banks to pay excessive interest on time deposits and has many times over again brought banks into serious trouble."[44] But the sudden appearance of this provision suggests some political motivation for deposit insurance. Considering that interest on deposits was a major cost of doing business, commercial banks may have viewed the measure as a necessary quid pro quo for their contributions to the FDIC.

In 1935, Congress extended federal authority (through the FDIC) to commercial banks outside the Federal Reserve System. In granting membership, the FDIC would henceforth consider "the convenience and needs of the community to be served." Criteria for chartering by the Comptroller and membership in the Federal Reserve System were similarly qualified; free entry—the hallmark of dual banking for nearly a century—had been curtailed.[45]

Early in the Hundred Days of the New Deal, while Senator Glass and his colleagues labored over banking legislation, Felix Frankfurter recruited three protégés to draft a federal securities law. These three "Happy Hot Dogs"—Thomas Corcoran, Benjamin Cohen, and James Landis—combined financial, legal, and administrative expertise in a mix well suited to their task.[46] From the first, financial disclosure for issuers of new corporate securities was at the heart of their work. This "sunshine" approach to the prevention of fraud and unethical financial practices was scarcely new, however; proposals for corporate disclosure, as a means of solving all sorts of industrial and corporate abuses, had been around since the 1880s. Most states already had enacted blue-sky laws to register publicly issued securities and to license brokers, but these measures had proved ineffective. (The model for many of these laws was the British Companies Act of 1900.)[47] Financial disclosure was supported, in principle, by the American Bankers Association, the Investment Bankers Association, and the accounting profession. Yet only the security industry's depressed condition, together with its obvious need to restore public confidence, transformed such vague support into concrete action.

On May 27, 1933, Congress passed the Securities Act as a compromise measure. It required the filing of a registration statement and the use of a prospectus for any public sale of securities. Issuers were liable to both criminal and civil penalties, and federal regulatory authorities received the subpoena power necessary to confirm accuracy of registration information.[48] Investment bankers not only resented the provisions for criminal liability but, as a practical matter, they objected most strenuously to the twenty-day "cooling off" period that Landis had designed to defuse the feverish, speculative atmosphere surrounding new issues.[49] According to the industry this delay would exacerbate risk, since market conditions often changed enough to endanger an issue. Reform-minded New Dealers, however, felt that the act was inadequate. "There is nothing in the Act," complained William O. Douglas, "which would control the speculative craze of the American public."[50]

The Senate, meanwhile, had been investigating brokerage practices and the operations of major exchanges. In 1933, the Banking Committee concluded that "federal regulation was necessary and desirable" because of the "evils and abuses which flourished on the exchanges and their disastrous effects upon the entire Nation."[51] Exchanges were too important and too much "affected with the public interest" to leave entirely to the discretion of members.[52] At the president's behest, Commerce Secretary Daniel Roper appointed a committee charged with finding a way to regulate exchanges by using "broad discretionary authority" that would not undermine "initiative and responsibility." This committee, whose members included James Landis and A. A. Berle, recommended a form of regulation that would be used to "supplement and supervise what in the first instance was self-regulation."[53]

James Landis took the lead in drafting the legislation that Senator Duncan Fletcher introduced in February 1934. Reactions to the early drafts, however, were largely negative. The business community generally, and the securities industry especially, felt that the draft legislation far exceeded any reasonable level of government intervention.[54] One section in particular, Sec. 18(c), authorized the Securities Commission "to prescribe such rules and regulations for national securities exchanges [and] their members . . . as it may deem necessary or appropriate in the public interest."[55] Richard Whitney, then president of the New York Stock Exchange (NYSE), complained that this section was more than regulation because it gave "the Commission power to manage exchanges and dictate brokerage practices."[56]

The Securities Exchange Act, as passed by Congress later in 1934, represented a compromise between regulation and self-regulation; it created a five-member, bipartisan Securities and Exchange Commission (SEC) to implement the Securities Act (and subsequently, the Public Utilities Holding Company Act of 1935 and the Investment Company Act of 1940). It had three substantive objectives: first, to extend federal control over credit in securities markets by authorizing the Federal Reserve Board to set margin rules and interest rates; second, to extend disclosure to securities brokers and impose a set of rules aimed at preventing manipulation of stock prices and fraudulent trading practices; and third, to provide supervision over the self-regulation of securities markets, particularly the practices of organized exchanges.[57]

The Securities Exchange Act provided latitude for the SEC in creating a flexible body of rules; over the next several years, with Landis himself as a commissioner and Joseph Kennedy as chairman, it enlisted accounting professionals to create standards for financial reporting, while the exchanges themselves began to implement rules for membership, trading, and brokerage fees.[58]

In 1938, the Maloney Act authorized the formation of an association of over-the-counter brokers and dealers, with antitrust immunity. Both the SEC and the organized exchanges supported this legislation. "To leave the over-the-counter markets out of a regulatory system," cautioned the Twentieth Century Fund, "would be to destroy the effects of regulating the organized exchanges."[59] At the time, stabilization of securities markets represented both a public and a private objective. Brokers and dealers organized the National Association of Securities Dealers (NASD) to establish trading standards and minimum fees. Abstainers would suffer the competitive disadvantage of exclusion from the trading network.

Investment funds stood next in line for federal control. After sustaining deep losses in the early 1930s (estimated by Senator Robert Wagner at $3 billion on total assets of $7 billion), "mutual funds" (open-ended investment trusts) had begun growing again.[60] The SEC, meanwhile, completed a four-year study of investment funds in 1939, and its recommendations formed the basis of the Investment Company Act of 1940.[61] This act required registration and detailed financial disclosure, further separation of fund management from other financial entities, and SEC regulation of selling practices, capital structure, and accounting practices.[62]

Within the financial services sector, only insurance companies had so far escaped the imposition of federal regulation. Because of loose state supervision, the practice of price fixing by private-rate bureaus soon became widespread; immunity from antitrust persecution was taken for granted. In 1944, however, the Supreme Court ruled that insurance contracts were interstate commerce and that price fixing violated the Sherman Act.[63] Under intense pressure from the insurance industry and its state regulators, Congress hastily approved the McCarran-Ferguson Act, which President Roosevelt signed in March 1945. This act endorsed the status quo and provided temporary immunity from federal antitrust authority. Although its legislative history suggests that Congress favored competition, the law practically assured cartelization.[64] Eventually forty-four states adopted "prior-approval laws" that authorized coordinated rate setting for liability insurance under state supervision.[65] And with these laws, the period of major financial reforms was complete.

Taken together, these reforms virtually ended competition in financial services. Product portfolios (assets) were restricted, sourcing of funds (liabilities) was allocated, geographic markets were segmented, prices were fixed, and operating practices were standardized. A stable, secure (and inefficient) financial system was the result.

REGULATION-DEFINED MARKETS

Today the U.S. financial services market, shaped by this regulatory regime for more than forty years, is unique in its size, diversity of products, and range of institutions. Over six trillion dollars of private financial assets are handled by more than 50,000 firms. These range from credit unions with a few thousand dollars in assets, to the largest money-center banks that hold over $100 billion in assets. Together, these intermediaries account for 15 percent of the gross national product; Table 2-2 provides a breakdown of the major asset holdings of these financial institutions.

Yet until very recently, this national financial system probably had changed less than any other sector of the American economy. A time traveler from 1935, as Benjamin Friedman has observed, would easily recognize the different types of financial institutions and understand their principal activities.[66] A closer look at Table 2-2, however, does suggest a few long-term trends: commercial banking still dominates financial services, but now it has only a third (not a half) of the market; insurance (primarily life insurance) also has lost half of its market share, although the industry's total assets have grown tenfold; thrifts (S&Ls), institutional investors (pension and money market funds), and the government stand out as sectors of high growth.

In banking, where regulation has been most pervasive, growth, profitability, and industry structure have remained amazingly stable for nearly forty years. Bank failures are the exception, thanks primarily to federal deposit insurance; fewer banks failed in the years between 1934 and 1978 than in any year during the 1920s.[67] Figures 2-1 and 2-2 show the trends for earnings and costs of all depository institutions.

In commercial banking, where entry, price, and product com-

Total Private Financial Assets: Percent Held by Different Financial Services Sectors
($ billions)

	1950		1960		1970		1980		1984	
	$Vol	%Mkt	$Vol	%Mkt	$Vol	%Mkt	$Vol	%Mkt	$Vol	%Mkt
Depository Institutions										
Commercial Banks	149.6	50.6	228.3	37.4	504.9	36.7	1,360.9	35.4	2,012.9	32.5
Thrifts										
Savings and Loans	16.9	5.7	71.5	11.7	176.2	12.8	629.8	16.4	989.9	15.9
Mutual Savings Banks	22.4	7.6	41.0	6.7	79.7	5.8	173.0	4.5	206.4	3.3
Credit Unions	1.0	0.3	6.3	1.0	18.0	1.3	69.6	1.8	115.8	1.9
Nondepository Institutions										
Insurance Companies	74.3	25.2	142.0	23.3	250.8	18.2	633.5	16.5	932.9	15.0
Securities Brokers and Dealers	4.0	1.3	6.7	1.1	16.2	1.2	34.6	0.9	60.5	0.9
Investment Funds										
Open-End Investment Companies	3.3	1.1	17.0	2.8	47.6	3.5	47.3	1.2	161.9	2.6
Private Pension Funds	7.1	2.4	38.2	6.2	110.4	8.0	264.8	6.9	623.4	10.0
Money Market Funds	0.0	0.0	0.0	0.0	0.0	0.0	78.4	2.0	209.7	3.4
Real Estate Investment Trusts (REIT's)	0.0	0.0	0.0	0.0	0.9	0.1	6.8	0.2	4.7	0.1
Miscellaneous										
Finance Companies	9.2	3.1	27.6	4.5	64.0	4.7	180.1	4.7	294.1	4.7
State and Local Gov. Retirement Funds	4.9	1.7	19.7	3.2	60.3	4.4	200.4	5.2	354.9	5.7
Federal Agencies and Mortgage Pools	3.2	1.1	11.5	1.9	46.5	3.4	165.1	4.3	249.1	4.0
Total	$295.9	100.0%	$609.7	100.0%	$1,375.5	100.0%	$3,844.3	100.0%	$6,216.2	100.0%

Note: Some figures are rounded off.
Source: The Board of Governors of the Federal Reserve System, Flow of Funds Accounts, various dates.

Figure 2-1
Asset Earning Rates and Market Interest Rates

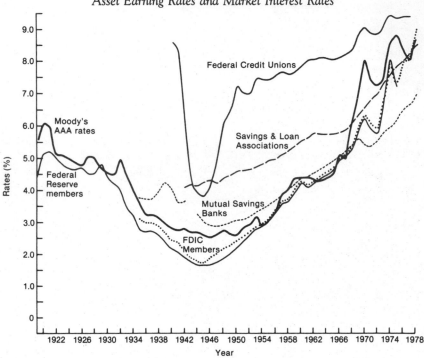

petition were restricted by regulation, rivalry for deposits and retail lending in the domestic market focused on branching. While the number of banks remained almost constant, the number of branches grew exponentially (see Figure 2-3). Over the years, state branching restrictions gradually eased (Table 2-3), as little evidence of monopoly profit or diminution of services emerged.[68]

Ironically, restrictions on holding companies gradually became more severe, even though the relative importance of the holding companies declined until the late 1960s.[69] In 1956, Congress enacted the Bank Holding Company Act to expand significantly the authority of the Federal Reserve System; coverage was extended to all multibank holding companies and not just the member banks. The act established new standards for acquisition of a bank by a holding company, and it prohibited interstate acquisitions. Most important, it prohibited bank hold-

Figure 2-2
Total Operating Costs per Deposit Dollar

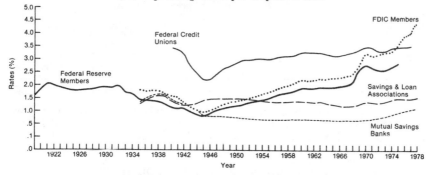

Source: Lewis J. Spellman, *The Depository Firm and Industry* (New York: Academic Press, 1982), pp. 175, 185.

Figure 2-3
Commercial Banks in the United States
Number, by Class
Call Report Dates

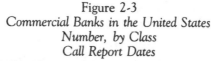

Commercial Banks in the United States
Number, by Class
Call Report Dates

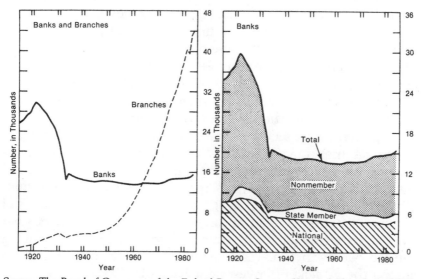

Source: The Board of Governors of the Federal Reserve System, *Historical Chart Book* (1985), p. 82.

Table 2-3
State Restrictions on Intrastate Branch Banking
(number of states and percentages)

Classification	1929	%	1951	%	1961	%	1983	%
Branching prohibited	28	58	17	35	16	32	8	16
Branching permitted but geographically limited	11	23	14	30	15	30	18	36
Unlimited branching	9	19	17	35	19	38	24	48
	48	100	48	100	50	100	50	100

Sources: Compiled from statistics of the American Bankers Association and the Board of Governors of the Federal Reserve System.

ing companies from engaging in nonfinancial activities, and it sharply circumscribed nonbank financial activities. Under the act, nonbank activities "of a financial, fiduciary, or insurance nature" were allowed only when they were "so closely related to the business of banking or managing or controlling banks as to be a proper incident thereto."[70]

Later, to reinforce the government's control over the structure of banking, Congress enacted the Bank Merger Act of 1960 in answer to pressures from the Comptroller, the Federal Reserve, and the FDIC. This act gave bank regulators exclusive authority over mergers and acquisitions, irrespective of competitive factors or the antitrust laws. Although it was soon overturned by the Supreme Court, the act was designed to insulate decisions of bank regulators from Justice Department oversight.[71] In 1966, Congress amended both the Merger and the Holding Company acts to impose a competitiveness test for the approval of mergers by bank regulators. When taken together, all of these structural controls were designed to maintain banking stability against the competitive pressures for change.

Similarly, in the securities trading and brokerage sector, regulatory stabilization lasted about 30 years before competitive pressures became overwhelming. The volume of securities issued and traded grew slowly, and with surprising stability, until the mid-1960s (see Figures 2-4 and 2-5). Industry leadership, in terms of market share and concentration, was also fairly stable. All but five of the twenty largest investment banks in 1965 were among the top twenty in 1935, and of these five banks three had been among the 30 leading investment banks in 1935.[72]

This structural stability was facilitated by the SEC's deference (despite its regulatory authority) to the anticompetitive mem-

Figure 2-4
Dollar Volume of Securities Issued,
1934–1980

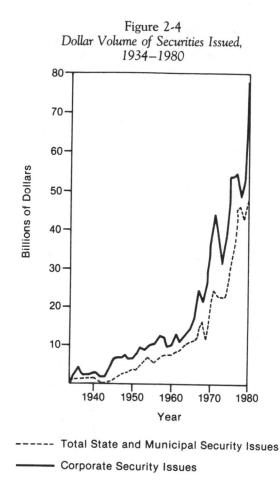

----- Total State and Municipal Security Issues

——— Corporate Security Issues

bership rules of the National Association of Securities Dealers (NASD), and the organized exchanges (especially the New York Stock Exchange). Four rules were particularly important. First, there were minimum brokerage commissions, which the New York Stock Exchange (NYSE) had maintained ever since the Buttonwood Tree Agreement of 1792. A flat-rate commission structure cross-subsidized small transactions (by individual investors) at the expense of large ones (by institutional investors).[73] This not only stifled price competition by exchange members, but also prevented nonmembers from using the exchange as a wholesale market.

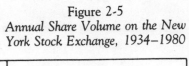

Figure 2-5
Annual Share Volume on the New
York Stock Exchange, 1934–1980

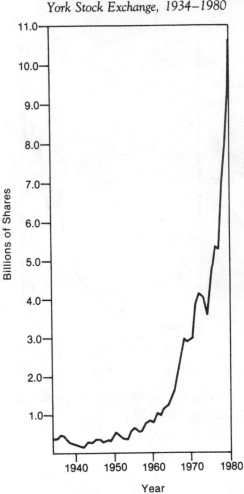

Year

Source: S. Hayes, et al., *Competition in the Investment Banking Industry* (Cambridge, Mass.:
Harvard University Press, 1983), p. 25.

To maintain this separation, a second rule prohibited commission splitting between members and nonmembers. Conversely, a third rule prohibited NYSE members from taking their customers' orders for an exchange-listed stock to the over-the-counter market (where volume discounts were available). And fourth, exchange membership was denied to any publicly held corporation. This prevented institutional investors and other financial services "customers" from integrating forward to capture the artificially high commissions on large transactions. [74]

These measures for implementing stability in commercial banking and securities, together with similar controls for thrifts, funds, and insurance, were developed and maintained by an elaborate network of federal and/or state regulatory bureaucracies. Seven federal agencies and various state banking and insurance commissions shared responsibility for controlling prices, guiding industry structure, defining product portfolios, and segmenting service markets (see Figure 2-6).

The most interesting organizational aspect of this system is the overlapping jurisdiction and political competition between the three major banking bureaucracies. Besides the normal interagency rivalries so common in Washington, there are other differences among them, not the least of which are their disagreements over the ranking of such priorities as an efficient banking system, a safe and stable system, and a system amenable to the exercise of monetary policy.

The oldest of these federal agencies, the Office of the Comptroller of the Currency (OCC), has 3,000 employees in its Washington and fourteen regional offices. The Comptroller, who is appointed by the president and affiliated with the Treasury Department, generally represents the administration's banking policies. The OCC regulates 4,800 nationally chartered banks with regard to new charters, mergers, branching, consumer-law compliance, prudential limits, soundness examinations, and international matters.

The Federal Deposit Insurance Corporation (FDIC) is a fully funded, quasi-autonomous corporation whose chairman is appointed by the president. The FDIC is primarily responsible for administering the deposit-insurance program, arranging mergers that arise from the need to avoid bank failures, and when necessary, conducting bankruptcy proceedings. The FDIC is also re-

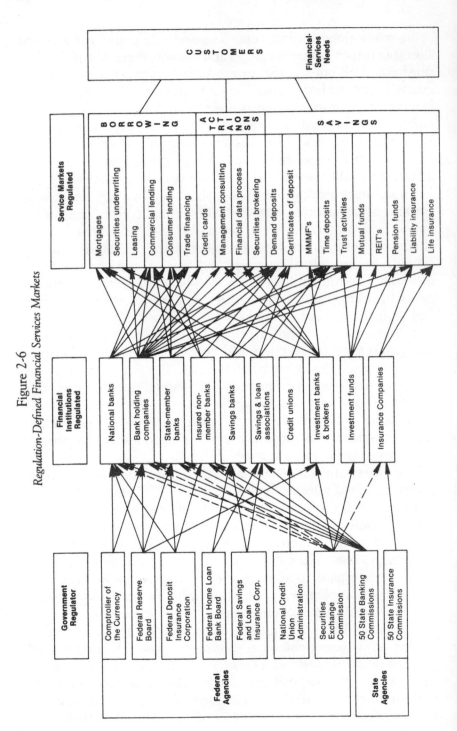

Figure 2-6
Regulation-Defined Financial Services Markets

sponsible for the general supervision of those banks among the 8,600 commercial banks that it insures that are not nationally chartered and are not members of the Federal Reserve System. In this capacity, the chairman of the FDIC has exercised an important voice in the establishment of state-chartered banks.

Because of its primary responsibility for monetary policy, the Federal Reserve Board has become the most important and the most powerful of the three federal regulators. The Board supervises the 1,100 state-chartered banks that are members of the Federal Reserve System and sets discount rates and reserve requirements for all member banks. It also supervises acquisitions and the bank-related financial activities of all bank holding companies.[75] Finally, through Regulation Q, the Federal Reserve Board has control of interest rates on deposits of its member banks and, with the concurrence of the FDIC and the FHLBB, of all banks.

THE SOURCES OF CHANGE

No sooner had this elaborate system of regulation been implemented than market pressures for change began to mount. Yet the regulatory system remained unresponsive to the changing economic conditions, entrepreneurship, technological innovation, and new ideas.

Put simply, bureaucratic inertia and private vested interests prevented timely adjustment. Thus, by distorting competition (ostensibly for the public good) and creating gaps between cost and price, this system contained "the seeds of its own destruction."[76] After 1965, lenders and borrowers increasingly bypassed normal financial channels in their attempts to avoid unnecessary costs or to capture "regulatory rents."[77] As they did so, competitive pressures intensified, regulated institutions began to fail, and new political alliances took shape around the issues of deregulation.

One fundamental source of change in this regulatory system was the shift in macroeconomic conditions that began in the mid-1960s. Stimulated by rapid economic growth, a high level of business investment, and increasing competition for deposits (as the prime route for asset growth allowed by regulation),

interest rates on deposits (and the ratio of time deposits to demand deposits) rose steadily between 1956 and 1965.[78] In 1966,
as government borrowing accelerated to finance the war in Viet-
nam, a credit crunch ensued; short-term rates exceeded both
long-term rates and the ceilings set under Regulation Q. Disintermediation (financial transactions that circumvent banks) and
an inverted yield curve resulted. For the thrift industry in particular this meant a decline in deposits and a squeeze on margins as
their short-term costs exceeded their long-term earnings.[79] As
short-term interest rates increased, so did bond yields.[80] Meanwhile, long-term corporate borrowing, led by the bond issues of
rapidly expanding utilities, intensified. In equity markets, the
volume of trading increased dramatically, as new institutional
investors sought to maximize their returns.[81]

In the longer term, slower economic growth and a decline in
the aggregate savings rate had a dampening impact on the supply
and demand for funds. Among other things, slower growth
intensified competition for market share in financial services.
Large government deficits and oil-price shocks in 1973 and 1979
contributed to the inflationary pressures that caused nominal
interest rates to reach new heights periodically throughout the
1970s. Also important were developments in international
finance. Floating exchange rates and petrodollar imbalances after 1973 accelerated the integration of global capital markets
that eventually helped undermine the artificial segmentation of
the regulatory status quo. These changes reverberated through
the financial markets. Further, more serious bouts of disintermediation and inverted yields followed in 1969, 1970, 1974,
1979, and 1981 (Figures 2-7 and 2-8).

In response to these developments, financial innovation was a
second source of change. Where regulatory constraints were especially binding, or where loopholes opened opportunities to
breach geographic or functional segmentation, the most aggressive firms devised new products and organizational innovations.
Among the earliest examples of these innovations was the negotiable certificates of deposit (CD's) that Citibank created in
1961 when its ability to attract deposits fell behind its loan
demand. A decade later, mutual banks in Massachusetts in-
vented negotiable order of withdrawal (NOW) accounts to
compete with commercial banks for checkable deposits. At the

Figure 2-7
Three-month Treasury Bill Rates and Regulation Q Ceilings

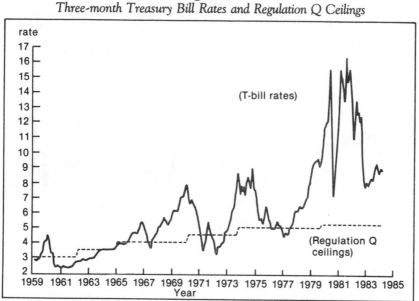

same time, the securities industry created money market mutual funds (MMMF's) to breach the Glass-Steagall Act and take advantage of the growing pressures for disintermediation.[82]

Over time, the bank holding company became an important organizational innovation that captured new economies of scale in data processing and circumvented the McFadden Act, the Glass-Steagall Act, and Regulation Q. The growth of these holding companies accelerated beginning in 1966—especially the growth of one-bank holding companies, which were exempted from regulation by the 1956 Bank Holding Company Act. As of 1965 there were 550 one-bank holding companies, and 891 more were created by the end of 1970. Even after the 1970 amendments to the Holding Company Act extended regulation to one-bank companies, more than 800 more were formed during the next eight years.[83] Most of these were intended to facilitate expansion into nondepository financial services; between 1971 and 1977 the Federal Reserve Board received requests for approval for nearly 700 acquisition proposals and more

Figure 2-8
Change in S&L Total Deposits

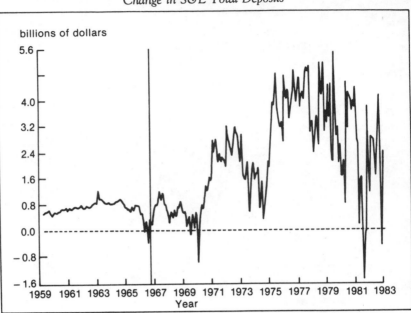

Note: The vertical line represents the extension of Regulation Q to S&Ls in
     September 1966.

Source: Reprinted from FINANCIAL REFORM IN THE 1980s by Thomas F. Cargill and
Gillian G. Garcia, with permission of Hoover Institution Press. © 1985 by the Board of Trustees
of the Leland Stanford Jr. University, pp. 82–83.

than 3,300 de novo ventures by bank holding companies, in
every conceivable "closely-related area" (Table 2-4).

New technology also worked to destabilize the regulated
financial system; information processing and telecommunications capabilities dramatically affected both supply and demand
for financial services and transaction products, and industry operations and structure. This revolution began in back office operations with the introduction of mainframe computers for data
processing and reader/sorter document processors and data re-
trieval systems that enhanced these computational capabilities.
With the development of digital (rather than analog/voice)
transmission capabilities, the revolution spread from headquar-
ters to branch-office integrated networks, and later into
wholesale operations—commercial lending, interbank transactions, and international banking—via electronic funds transfers. During the past ten years, new technology has reached

Table 2-4
*Federal Reserve Board Actions on Nonbanking
Acquisitions of Bank Holding Companies,
1971–1977*

Type of Firm	De novo Notifications Received	Proposed Acquisitions Processed by Board		
		Total Received	Approved	Denied
Fiduciary and trust	60	15	14	1
Mortgage banking	475	107	83	10
Leasing	403	30	17	3
Investment, financial, and economic advisory services	196	17	13	3
Insurance agency or broker	956	177	129	15
Insurance underwriting Credit life, accident, and health	66	65	50	0
Finance company				
General	287	7	4	0
Commercial	104	7	13	0
Consumer	523	123	96	9
Insurance premium	6	6	5	0
Mobile homes	0	5	2	2
Agricultural	6	4	3	1
Data processing	130	30	20	1
Factoring	47	12	8	1
Community development	20	5	0	2
Industrial banking	59	21	15	3
Management consulting for banks	1	12	11	0
Savings and loan association	0	5	2	3
Other	16	22	12	0
Total	3,355	670	497	54

Source: C. A. Glassman and R. A. Eisenbeis, "Bank Holding Companies and Concentration of Banking and Financial Resources," in *The Bank Holding Company Movement to 1978: A Compendium*, the Board of Governors of the Federal Reserve System (Washington, D.C., 1978), p. 255.

into the "front office" (retail markets) with the development
of point-of-sale (POS) terminals, automated teller machines
(ATM's), as well as magnetic, electron, and "smart" cards for
credit and debit transactions; and now home information systems are on the horizon.[84]

The impact of these innovations on operations and competition is a story in itself. Besides the more obvious effects on retail
distribution and new product development, these technological
changes have had a fundamental effect on the economics and
structure of the financial services industry and its regulation.
Electronic funds transfers (EFT), in both the front and back
office, have created significant new economies of scale and,
especially, of scope. EFT technology reduces unit costs through
scale economies of large systems; but the scope economies of
spreading production and distribution costs across a broad line of
electronic transactions are even more significant. These economies, together with the physical attributes of EFT systems, lower
the barriers to arbitrage across the two key regulatory boundaries—product and geographic segmentation. On the product
side, as Edward Kane explains it, EFT technology "allows management to coordinate unregulated substitute arrangements such
as sweep accounts or the activities of an array of subsidiary
firms," and thus, with product line homogenization more likely,
"exclusionary rules would tend to lose their effectiveness."[85]
With respect to geographic segmentation, EFT has decimated
cost barriers, as illustrated by the following EFT service innovations: automated teller machines (which have completely undermined the traditional structure of intrastate branch banking),
multifunctional nationwide credit card services, brokerage services that reach beyond traditional money centers, and direct
(nonagency) insurance sales.[86]

New ideas about the causes of the Great Depression, and
about the original justifications for regulation and the political
desirability of government regulation, have transformed these
economic and business developments into public policy issues.

Research since the mid-1960s, especially in economic history
and industrial organization, has provided mounting evidence
that integrated financial service firms neither caused the collapse
of the banking system nor had a higher failure rate than unit

banks or private investment houses.[87] Research has also shown that the concept of *excess* competition, at least as it relates to banking (in terms of interest on deposits), securities (fixed brokerage fees and restrictive membership rules), and insurance (price-fixing bureaus), holds little of substance.[88] Moreover, structural analysis of branching, interstate banking, and bank holding companies reveals no unwarranted propensity toward concentration or the flight of capital from rural communities to money-center banks.[89]

Much of this analysis has contributed to the broad reassessment of economic regulation in which economists such as Kahn, Stigler, Phillips, and MacAvoy have demonstrated the inefficiency of economic regulation. Other specialists, such as political scientists, historians, and legal scholars, have attacked regulation for its inequity and ineffectiveness. Such intellectual criticisms took root in the political arena during the Nixon administration and then blossomed during the Ford and Carter years.[90] So by the time the Reagan administration declared deregulation an article of faith, Congress had already enacted legislation that had substantially deregulated half a dozen different industries.[91]

The final (and the most direct) source of change was the failure of regulation itself; it was not just the inefficiency, but also the gross distortions and discontinuities that simply undermined the regulatory status quo. Once imbalances become severe enough, disintermediation, or the bypassing of regulated institutions by customers and their use of close substitutes, generally forces the issue. The uprising of institutional investors against the fixed commission rates of the NYSE, the incredible success of money market funds, the failure of major banks like Continental Illinois (despite deposit insurance) due to "wire-runs" by large depositors, and the S&L crisis of the early 1980s all dramatically illustrate this phenomenon.

Acting together, these important forces of change created new pressures on the prevailing structure of political interests. As the political organization of economic interests realigned, the process of administrative and legislative reform gained momentum. In financial services, however, this reform process has been relatively slow and halting.

REGULATORY REFORM

In 1974, according to a report by the National Association of Insurance Commissioners, "the insurance industry [was] earnestly advocating the enactment of open competition laws . . . a classic reversal of historical position."[92] Pressure for change had come initially from direct insurers (companies that both underwrote and sold automobile and homeowners insurance). Companies such as Allstate and State Farm had grown rapidly during the 1960s by using their lower distribution costs to underprice competitors. But they needed freedom from the rate bureaus; eventually, they were joined by other low-cost underwriters that wanted rates more responsive to inflation and loss experience.[93] As inflation drove insurance rates higher in the late 1960s, state regulators also grew dissatisfied with the system of prior approval. Although the property-liability sector appeared to have excess capacity, the inflexible pricing that was tied to standard, average operating margins contributed to localized shortages of various types of higher-risk coverage. Yet the industry's return on net worth was still lower than either industrials or utilities.[94]

In the face of this gradually deteriorating performance, regulators turned increasingly to the only available example of competition, the industry in California, for solutions. California had never adopted the prior-approval model of regulation, and although rate bureaus existed to pool risk data, nearly half the companies in California offered prices below bureau rates. And yet the frequency of insurance failure was no greater than elsewhere. Accordingly, the state of New York adopted a competitive-pricing law in 1969, on a four-year trial basis. Regulation of maximum rates and discrimination within the industry continued, but concerted rate fixing by the companies was declared illegal.

None of the worst fears materialized during the trial period in New York. The industry, after all, already had some characteristics of a competitive industry: a low level of concentration, low-entry barriers, a shared distribution system, and few economies of scale. There was no reason why insurance markets should not be "contestable."[95] Prices, in fact, did not fly up, profits did not increase (relative to other states), and the industry did not become significantly more concentrated. Instead, prices started

Figure 2-9

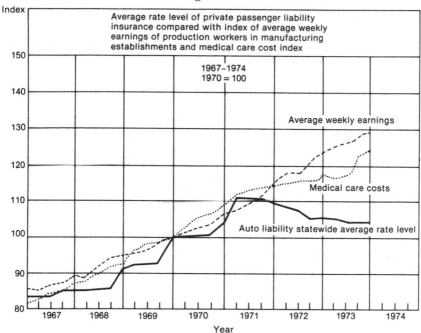

Source: New York State Insurance Department, *Cartels vs. Competition: A Critique of Insurance Price Regulation* (New York, 1975), p. 16.

falling in real terms (Figures 2-9 and 2-10), while the rate of nominal increases dropped well below those of prior-approval states. Availability also improved, as did product quality.[96]

The success of this experiment in so prominent a state as New York led to a wave of conversions to competitive rate making. By 1984 seventeen states used "open-competition" rate making under regulatory supervision. In a few states, such as Massachusetts, the state regulatory agency set rates; in most other states, insurers still operated rate bureaus, but could deviate from their rates with the regulator's approval. Yet only in Illinois (since 1971), was the pricing of property-liability insurance fully deregulated; elsewhere, regulation still prevailed.[97]

The process of regulatory reform in the securities industry took more than ten years and was accomplished only after repeated judicial challenges, pressure from the Justice Department, the development of serious performance problems, and finally, congressional scrutiny and criticism. The SEC was hesi-

Figure 2-10

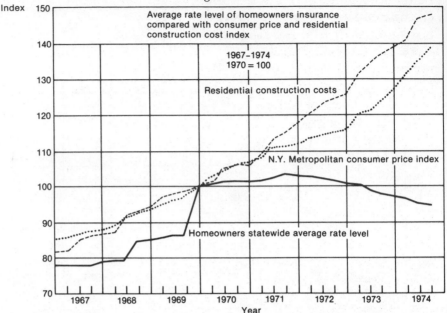

Source: New York State Insurance Department, *Cartels vs. Competition: A Critique of Insurance Price Regulation* (New York, 1975), p. 22.

tant to press for change, and the New York Stock Exchange generally opposed it. It was the growth of institutional investors and their attacks on the system of fixed commission rates and the NYSE's web of exclusionary rules that brought about changes.

Between 1960 and 1968, the daily volume of trading on the New York Stock Exchange grew from 3 million to 21 million shares (see Figures 2-4 and 2-5). Institutional investors, especially insurance companies, mutual funds, and pension funds, accounted for about 50 percent of that growth.[98] Despite this volume increase, the system of noncompetitive commission rates remained virtually unchanged. The volume component of commission rates was uniform; the share-price component was not. Thus, the fee for a sale of one thousand shares of a stock was ten times that for a sale of one hundred shares of the same stock, but the commission for a trade of ten shares of a $50 stock was larger than that for a trade of ten shares of a $5 stock. Obviously, neither schedule bore any relationship to cost, and both discriminated (in economic terms) against the large transactions of institutional investors.[99]

To avoid these excessive fees, institutional investors and their nonmember brokers first challenged, and then bypassed, the NYSE's exclusionary rules. For example, Rule 394, which prohibited members of the exchange from buying or selling listed securities off the exchange, first came under attack in 1964. A nonmember broker who had lost his business in the stock of Chase Manhattan Bank after it was listed threatened to bring suit against the NYSE. After the broker complained to the Senate Subcommittee on Antitrust, the SEC staff recommended that the rule be modified by allowing members to buy or sell over-the-counter when OTC dealers offered a better price. But the SEC, faced with adamant opposition from Wall Street, rejected its staff's recommendation and eventually implemented only a minor, narrowly written change that made little difference.[100]

For many institutional investors, exchange membership would have been the next best solution. Indeed, several of the regional exchanges sought to grow by attracting institutional investors. But the NYSE, where 96 percent of the common stock holdings of institutional investors were listed, prohibited institutional membership under Rule 318, which required members to be privately held. Even when this rule was later modified in 1969 to allow member brokers to raise growth capital, a new provision was added requiring members to earn at least 50 percent of gross income from broker-dealer activities.[101]

Not surprisingly, a group of investment companies had already sued the NYSE and four member firms in 1966, alleging conspiracy in restraint of trade (Section 1 of the Sherman Act) through price fixing. Although the case was dismissed on the grounds that the SEC did have the authority to fix "reasonable" rates, Chief Justice Earl Warren dissented because he sensed a discrepancy between "the Exchange's rate-fixing practice . . . [and] this nation's commitment . . . to competitive pricing."[102] This signal seemed clear enough to the Justice Department, if not to the SEC.

Pressures to economize, by means of "give ups" or "fee splitting," intensified. When making large trades through the NYSE,

institutional investors insisted that exchange-member brokers
"give up" part of the commission, as an indirect rebate, to another broker who handled the investor's own stock (if a mutual
fund) or provided research and consultative services. These
"give ups" amounted to 38 percent of commission fees from
investment companies in 1968, when the SEC finally moved to
close that loophole. Today, it remains unclear whether the
SEC's ruling (10b-10) was intended to support the structure of
commission rates or to put additional pressure on it by highlight-
ing the absurd.[103]

The Antitrust Division of the Justice Department chose April
Fools' Day, 1968, to put the issue of deregulation squarely on the
table. In a long statement on the SEC's proposed rules against
"give ups," the Justice Department flatly called for abolition of
fixed commission rates and new means "for assuring equitable
and non-discriminatory access . . . to the NYSE market."[104] If
the price fixing were abolished, argued the Justice Department,
the problems with institutional investors and Rule 394 would be
substantially dissipated. This initiative forced both the NYSE
and the SEC to engage the issue, and, eventually, both responded.

In the meantime, Wall Street was struck by a paperwork
crisis. The absence of significant competitive pressures had,
among other things, relieved most securities firms from any need
to modernize their back office operations with data processing
and communications systems. In 1963 the SEC had issued a
prophetic warning "that present securities handling, clearing,
and delivery methods would prove inadequate to meet any sustained increase in volume."[105] When trading volume did jump
to 21 million shares daily in 1968, Wall Street was caught flat-
footed. "Fails" (the inability to implement transactions in time)
multiplied, even though the brokerage firms hired and trained
clerks as fast as possible; when the market turned down in 1969,
this excess overhead resulted in average losses of 2.9 percent on
security commissions. More than one hundred brokers were
forced into liquidation, and Congress reacted by passing the
Securities Investor Protection Act of 1970.[106]

The NYSE responded to these growing pressures by suggesting
a new rate structure, still regulated, but more in line with costs.
And the SEC finally proposed free commissions on transactions

larger than $100,000. With this first step, the pace of change accelerated. The SEC published its *Institutional Investor Study* in 1971, acknowledging that fixed commission rates on large transactions were "the source of a number of difficulties." One month later fixed rates on orders larger than $500,000 were abolished. Then, following a policy of "prudent gradualism," the SEC successively lowered the break-points for competitive rates throughout 1974. Meanwhile, the Senate Banking Committee completed a major investigation of securities markets and concluded that regulation, although "essential" for protecting investors, was "not an effective substitute for competition."[107] With the Justice Department threatening to bring suit to override the SEC and with incessant political pressure from the American Bankers Association, the Life Insurance Association of America, and Investors Diversified Services, the resistance to competition finally crumbled. The SEC announced an end to fixed commission rates, as of May 1, 1975.

Thereafter, commission rates plummeted on large trades, the average size of trades increased, and trading volume ballooned (from 37 in 1975 to 51 million average daily shares by 1980). As prices moved toward cost, product lines were unbundled, and the discount brokerage business took off.[108] By 1980, more than 70 discount brokers, led by Charles Schwab, held 9 percent of market share, and profits for the whole securities industry were never better. In 1980, a record year, the securities industry's after-tax return was 20 percent—nearly twice the earnings of banks and bank holding companies. Not surprisingly, these profits and the opportunity for functional and geographic expansion attracted new entrants, especially from banking, since the Glass-Steagall Act evidently did not prohibit brokerage per se (as it did underwriting).[109]

In the thrift and commercial banking sectors, price regulation (in the form of interest-rate ceilings on deposits) broke down first under crisis conditions; geographic and product restrictions disintegrated more gradually and still remain in some areas.

The process of price deregulation began (perversely) during the credit crunch of 1966. The Federal Reserve Board asked Congress for greater discretion to set rate ceilings under Regulation Q for the different categories of time deposits. To curb competition for deposits, the Federal Reserve also asked that the

FHLBB and FDIC, in consultation with the Board, be authorized to set interest-rate ceilings for S&Ls and mutual savings banks. Congress obliged with the Interest Rate Control Act of 1966.[110]

In subsequent periods of yield inversion and disintermediation, the Federal Reserve tried without success to "tune" the ceiling structure for different categories of deposits. But the types of regulated accounts proliferated, from two in 1965 to twenty-four by 1979. When banks offered consumer-type CD's, the Federal Reserve imposed rate ceilings. Then, when rising interest rates in the market threatened the CD's controlled under Regulation Q, big banks turned to foreign borrowing, interbank funds, and repurchase agreements. Mutual savings banks, as mentioned, created NOW accounts, and S&Ls turned to non-price methods of competition. Free checking accounts and other giveaways (toasters, can openers, and umbrellas) were the most obvious, but convenient parking, drive-in facilities, and rapid expansion of branches were more important.[111]

In 1973, when the interest rate gap between market rates and Regulation Q reached nearly 4 percent, the Federal Reserve gave in a little and suspended the rate ceiling on time deposits over $100,000. But this divergent treatment of large and small depositors only created new opportunities for disintermediation. Mutual funds, investing in CD's and commercial paper, could offer earnings higher-than-Q to small savers. The securities industry, recognizing this as an opportunity to breach the Glass-Steagall Act, created the Money Market Mutual Fund. Despite additional steps by the Federal Reserve to decontrol medium-size time deposits, money market funds had attracted $78 billion by 1980 and $209 billion by 1984.

Thrifts, unlike commercial banks, could not easily diversify their sources of funds through holding-company activities nor manage their assets to minimize interest-rate risk. State usury laws constrained asset earnings, and the Home Owners Equity Act of 1933 constrained asset mix.[112] With the inflation and disintermediation of 1973–1974, the earnings of S&Ls and mutual banks declined sharply. Then, after recovering briefly in the late 70s, return on equity nearly fell to zero in 1980. Only when regulation was obviously failing, did Congress finally act.

In March 1980 President Carter signed the Depository Institutions Deregulation and Monetary Control Act (DIDMCA). State usury laws were preempted, and interest-rate ceilings under Regulation Q were to be phased out over six years under the supervision of a committee of federal bank regulators (the Depository Institutions Deregulation Committee). For demand deposits, however, the zero-interest ceiling was retained. In addition to phasing out price controls, the act loosened product restrictions in an effort to make thrifts more competitive with commercial banks. S&Ls were authorized to issue NOW accounts and, on the asset side, to offer a wider range of mortgages, commercial real estate loans, and credit cards; mutual banks could even commit a small portion of assets to commercial loans. And to further underwrite deposit risk, federal deposit insurance was increased from $40,000 to $100,000.

DIDMCA, however, was not enough. High inflation, record-high interest rates, and rampant disintermediation persisted well into 1982 and pushed the entire thrift industry into crisis. Return on net worth plummeted to minus 16.9 percent; S&L net worth, after deducting unrealized mortgage claims, dropped to a negative $150 billion.[113] In 1981–1982, the FSLIC supervised 223 S&L mergers, of which 70 involved deposit insurance outlays of more than $900 million.[114] This time commercial banks also suffered; 52 banks, with $12 billion in insured deposits, failed between 1981 and 1982. Among these was Penn Square, which had sold its worthless, oil-related assets to such big city banks as Seafirst, Continental Illinois, and Chase Manhattan.

In something of a panic, Congress passed the Garn-St. Germain Depository Institutions Act of 1982; this law was clearly an emergency measure designed to relieve the thrift industry. The FDIC and the FSLIC were given much broader authority and discretion to bolster or bail out ailing institutions. These powers included making loans or guarantees, purchasing assets or liabilities, and most significantly, arranging mergers and acquisitions between thrifts and other financial institutions (including bank holding companies) that sometimes extended across state lines. Finally Congress had acknowledged the failure of its efforts to protect products and markets. On the liabilities side, S&Ls and savings banks were authorized to offer Super NOW accounts to a wider range of customers and to offer money market deposit accounts (MMDA's), with unrestricted interest rates and minimum balances of $2,500, in direct competition with MMMF's. On the asset side, thrifts were allowed to buy state and local securities and to expand their product lines into the commercial, consumer, and educational loan markets.[115]

In neither of these laws, however, did Congress explicitly address the issues of interstate banking or product-market restrictions on commercial banks and bank holding companies. As bank managers tested those restrictions for every conceivable weakness or loophole, it remained for bank regulators and the courts to mediate the progress of competition.

Already large banks were breaching some geographic barriers and generating loans through ingenious distribution channels. Regional offices permitted by the Edge Act serviced international accounts while loan production offices attracted domestic business. Cash management was performed nationally by growing networks of credit cards. The challenge to expand deposits proved more difficult; automatic teller machines (ATM's) helped, but only in intrastate markets. Third-party (or "shared") ATM networks held the potential for national deposit taking, but they were still prohibited by state laws. By 1985, three states had authorized unrestricted interstate banking, while a dozen more states were considering it. Regional compacts that were established in New England and the Southeast allowed reciprocal cross-border mergers but prevented entry by money-center banks.[116] In June 1985, the Supreme Court, turning aside a challenge by Citicorp, unanimously upheld regional reciprocity.[117] As regional mergers were consummated, some big banks like Bankers Trust abandoned the strategy of interstate retail expansion and refocused on the wholesale market in the manner of pre–1933 bank affiliates.

Even faster than geographic barriers, product line segmentation among banks and other financial service firms was dissolving. Technological innovations were nullifying entry barriers to commercial banking yet Congress refused to make any significant concessions in either the Glass-Steagall Act or Bank Holding Company Act restrictions. Less-regulated companies such as American Express, Prudential/Bache, Sears, and Merrill Lynch built on their electronic transactions capabilities to contrive products for bypassing commercial banks; Merrill Lynch's Cash Management Account was a prime example. Citibank's chairman, Walter Wriston, evinced his frustration with this one-way window when he observed that "the bank of the future already exists, and it's called Merrill Lynch."[118]

In fact, the "nonbank bank" appeared to offer commercial banks an escape route from the geographic and product line restrictions that had imprisoned them.[119] This route, after all, was the means by which securities, insurance, and other financial service firms had entered directly into the banking business. Yet when bank holding companies tried to reverse the flow and expand their activities in 1983, the nonbank bank (or so-called "loophole bank") became one more controversial symbol of the misfit between regulation and competition.

The Bank Holding Company Act defines a "bank" as any institution "which (1) accepts deposits that the depositor has a legal right to withdraw on demand, *and* (2) engages in the business of making commercial loans."[120] This two-part definition did not appear in the original act, which simply relied on a chartering test; the criteria of acceptance of demand deposits was added in 1966, and the *commercial* loan restriction, in 1970. Periodically during the 1970s, the Federal Reserve Board was called on to qualify and hone this definition further.[121] The reason for these efforts to tighten the definition can be found in the act itself, which was designed "to prevent the undue concentration of commercial banking activities" and "to maintain the traditional separation between banking and (commerce) in order to prevent abuses of allocation of credit."[122]

When is a bank not a bank? When an institution performs only half the normal functions of a bank, that is, it *either* accepts demand deposits *or* makes commercial loans (but does not do both), it is not a bank. In 1980, Gulf & Western's subsidiary, Associates First Capital Corporation, announced its intention to acquire Fidelity National Bank in California. Associates's application to the Comptroller of the Currency proposed divesting the bank's commercial loan portfolio, thereby removing the bank from the jurisdiction of the Federal Reserve Board. The Comptroller approved it, and the nonbank bank was born. By 1981, nonbank banks had started to multiply; small banks bought by Household Finance, Avco, and Parker Pen divested their commercial loan portfolios and became eligible for the Federal Reserve's check-clearing services and for FDIC insurance. Citicorp acquired a national charter for doing credit card business out of South Dakota, thus avoiding New York's usury laws.

At first (according to one former official) the Federal Reserve was "asleep at the switch." But in 1982, with de facto repeal of the Bank Holding Company Act under way, the Federal Reserve moved to block nonbank banks. To stop the takeover of Beehive Thrift and Loan by First Bankcorporation of Utah (a bank holding company), the Federal Reserve ruled that a NOW account was a demand deposit. Later that year, when Dreyfus Corporation (a manager of mutual funds) acquired Lincoln State Bank, which was chartered in New Jersey, the Federal Reserve objected; but the chairman of the FDIC asserted his power of jurisdiction and approved the acquisition.

In March 1983, Dimension Financial Corporation filed thirty-one nonbank bank applications with the Comptroller. These nonbank banks, planned for twenty-five states, would concentrate at first on providing trust services and large consumer loans, and would eventually engage in brokerage, insurance, tax planning, and other services—but not commercial loans. According to one congressional staffer, these "blatantly greedy" applications "scared a lot of people" and "mobilized Congress."[123] Jake Garn, chairman of the Senate Banking Committee, and Ferdinand St. Germain, chairman of the House Banking Committee, both expressed their concern over this widening loophole in bank regulation. The Federal Reserve, meanwhile, moved to broaden its definition of a bank to include an assortment of asset and liability transactions. Dimension Financial immediately challenged the Federal Reserve's authority in court. In an effort to help (force) Congress "foster free and open debate" of the broader issues of deregulation, Todd Conover, the Comptroller, announced a *temporary* moratorium on several hundred pending applications.

During the next two years, an intense and complicated political battle developed around the issue of nonbank banks. Hearings revealed deep differences within Congress, within the banking industry, and among the financial services sectors and bank regulators. Paul Volcker, speaking for the Federal Reserve Board, opposed deregulation via the nonbank bank, fearing loss of control over the money supply. Todd Conover and William Isaacs

(FDIC chairman), as spokesmen for the Reagan administration, defended the nonbank loophole as a lever to force Congress to deregulate rationally.[124] But the Independent Bankers Association, representing small and rural banks, and the Conference of State Bank Supervisors, claimed that the nonbank bank "lays waste to an entire body of public interest" by allowing "concentration of banking resources in the hands of a few financial giants."[125]

In 1985, when Representative St. Germain introduced legislation designed to close, not open, the nonbank loophole, Todd Conover terminated the moratorium and started approving applications. The Dimension Financial Corp. case, meanwhile, had worked its way to the Supreme Court. In January 1986, the Court ruled 8-0 in favor of Dimension. Chief Justice Burger argued that "there is much to be said for regulating financial institutions that are the functional equivalent of banks," but it is "a problem for Congress, and not the Board or the courts, to address."[126] But Congress found it difficult to design legislation that stayed ahead of market momentum.

REGULATION AND DEREGULATION IN PERSPECTIVE

By the mid-1980s, the boundaries of financial service markets were blurred beyond recognition. What had once been the carefully segmented domain of banks, thrifts, and securities firms now seemed crowded with industrial corporations such as General Electric, financial concerns such as American Express, insurance companies such as Prudential, and a host of retail companies, including Sears, K Mart, and Montgomery Ward. In fact, in 1983 the combined financial service earnings ($3 billion) of ten large nonfinancial-based firms was about the same as the combined total earnings of the three largest nonbank financial companies and the six largest bank holding companies.[127] A time traveler would by now have begun to experience some confusion.

After more than half a century, the regulation and deregulation of financial services now appear as part of a sweeping historical process, and not a mere collection of isolated incidents.

Most other industries that provide the economy's infrastructure—airlines, trucking, telecommunications, oil and natural gas—came under governmental regulation amidst the economic trauma of the 1930s. As soon as these regulatory regimes were implemented during the two high-growth decades after World War II, they too began to falter. By the mid-1970s, the markets and institutions defined by regulation were stagnating, unable to utilize new technologies or deliver gains in productivity. Collectively, these problems were part and parcel of slower growth in aggregate demand, inflation, and unemployment. Keynesian demand management, like regulation, no longer delivered on the public interest.

The process of regulatory reform, in other words, is a shifting balance that has to allocate economic goods through market and administrative means according to the distributive performance and institutional stability of each. Although this cycle is academic, the reasons for its onset, the impact of regulatory change on markets and industry structure, and the strategic responses of firms are not.

Regulation is a political solution to the failure of markets and institutions to serve the public interest. In financial services, the stock market crash and banking collapses were blamed on excess competition and horizontal integration. Similarly, the petroleum production controls of the Connelly Hot Oil Act of 1935 were the result of a simultaneous collapse in demand and extraordinary increase in oil discoveries. Telecommunications came under federal control in 1935 so as to regulate the Bell System's alleged natural monopoly in long-distance telephone service and to facilitate the spread of "universal service," which had come to be viewed as a public good. Trucking was curbed in 1935 and the airlines in 1938, both on the grounds of excess competition. Also in 1938, the Federal Power Commission took charge of interstate natural gas pipelines (another natural monopoly).

Regulation in each of these industries, as in financial services, appeared to work well enough until the mid-1960s, when basic economic conditions, political ideology, and technology began to change. By the mid-1970s, slower growth, oil prices, inflation, and record-high interest rates had aggravated frictions between the terms of regulation and the competitive dynamics of these regulated industries. In telecommunications, for example, electronic switching, microwave, satellites, and fiber optics diversified demand, undermined entry barriers, and created an opportunity for large customers to *bypass* the public switched network, wherever regulated prices exceeded costs to cross-subsidize universal service. This was the functional equivalent of disintermediation. In the airline industry, higher fuel costs, interest charges on investments in widebodied aircraft, extraordinary labor costs, and excess capacity (which led to higher prices under regulation), collided head-on with recessionary slumps in passenger traffic.

In all of these instances, business and political entrepreneurs were ready to take advantage of regulatory loopholes and market inefficiencies and entry opportunities. Bill McGowen, the founder and chairman of MCI Corporation, saw in microwave an opportunity to skim the cream off AT&T's private lines for intercity long-distance service (where prices were at least three times marginal costs). Lamar Muse, the CEO of Southwest Airlines, stuck to the unregulated, intercity markets in Texas in order to undercut the regulated majors with low-cost, high-density, point-to-point service. These were the entrepreneurial counterparts of Charles Schwab and Dimension Financial Corp.

The history of deregulation in financial services, as in all of these sectors, attests to the immense effects of regulatory change on market structure and the characteristics and relationships of buyers and sellers; market entry, market segmentation, pricing mechanisms, cost structure, vertical integration, and the boundaries of relevant markets all changed dramatically with deregulation. In perspective, of course, this should not be surprising, since regulation originally defined and shaped those characteristics on the basis of public policy premises.

Recent experience in airlines, trucking, and telecommunications has revealed the effects of regulation on entry, cost structure, and industry organization. Deregulation brought a rampant increase in new entries in each of these industries, usually by low-cost start-ups serving particular product or geographic niches. Partly because of this, but also because of increased competition among the incumbents, the price structure of deregulated services either stabilized or actually fell, and as a result, so did their costs; economic regulation, no matter how carefully implemented, had bred excess capacity, over-capitalization, high labor costs, unnecessary overhead, and inefficient operating systems. In the airlines industry, grounding aircraft, negotiating new labor contracts, reducing headcount, and restructuring routes (to hub-and-spoke) became brutal necessities. In telecommunications, headcount and overhead are still being reduced, in some cases by as much as 20–30 percent. In the railroad industry, thousands of employees are being bought out, tens of thousands of track miles are being abandoned, and hundreds of thousands of boxcars are being junked.

As a result of these and other changes, each of the industries being deregulated has experienced a massive organizational restructuring. Takeovers in the oil industry, where firms were so large and debt structures so modest, have illustrated this most vividly. But in airlines and in trucking, too, mergers, acquisitions, and bankruptcies have become commonplace. In the past ten years, thirty major railroads have been consolidated into seven regional systems; in telecommunications, a single court order shattered a century of organizational evolution.

Accompanying these revolutionary changes in markets were new alliances and reordered interests among the stakeholders in the political arena. All sorts of producers, buyers, suppliers, substitutes, potential entrants, social groups, and bureaucratic and administrative interests vied to shape the emerging regime to serve their vested interests. Deregulation is above all redistributive, and it is typically accompanied by intense political maneuvering for favorable legislation, administrative implementation, and judicial review.

Even now the process of deregulation in financial services is far from complete. Regulation of product lines, geographic markets, and industry structure is still in force, along with operational and fiduciary standards, and deposit insurance. And despite a quickening of mergers, acquisitions, and new ventures, the industry structure remains fundamentally fragmented and, in view of modern technology, anachronistic. If the deregulation experience of other industries is at all transferable, then further dramatic change in financial services is certain.

In the short run, the political process will be driven by pressures for reregulation and for compensating adjustments to problems caused by the transition itself. The term "reregulation" is used narrowly here to describe new legislative or regulatory initiatives, supported by specific interest groups under pressure from deregulation, that are designed to restrict competitive pressures in a particular product market or geographic segment. Interstate compacts are a good example, as is Representative St. Germain's efforts to close the nonbank loophole. Transitional regulations, however, are different in character and intent; they are generally regulatory responses to problems caused by the contradictions between regulation and competition and include such measures as new rules regarding mergers among failing banks, unified reserve requirements, safety and soundness (to protect against greater risk), and deposit insurance (in the face of cross subsidies).

In the longer run, the economic pressures already unleashed will continue to erode entry restrictions, artificial segmentation, and other loopholes and fuel the drive toward cost-based pricing and competitive equilibria. There is also a very considerable political momentum behind deregulation that is fueled by the positive results in other industries and by antigovernment ideologies. This process will only stop if at some point, as a result of some real market failure or a perceived public need, it is determined that banks *are* special. While the regulatory policies of the Great Depression were certainly an overreaction to market failure, there is no reason to think that the fundamental problems of excess risk and monetary instability no longer exist. It is still unclear, in telecommunications, in railroads, and even in airlines, whether or not some segment or function may remain susceptible to competitive failure and therefore in need of regulation.

These prospects, in light of the recent past, have several implications. In the short term, the management of financial service firms must not only track but also actively try to manage the process of regulatory change. Otherwise, short-sighted reregulation or distorted transitional policies may create significant competitive disadvantages that possess lasting effects. But more important, these short-run developments should not be allowed to obscure or confuse longer-run strategic adjustments to a less-regulated, more competitive environment. Financial service companies, especially in banking, need to anticipate the direction of deregulation and where it might stop; then they must act.

The record of winners and losers thus far would suggest that quick, decisive, and (if necessary) severe adjustment is the surest route to success.

NOTES

1. For a useful overview of the relationship between the financial markets and the government, see Benjamin Friedman, "Postwar Changes in the American Financial Markets," in *The American Economy in Transition,* ed. Martin Feldman (Chicago: University of Chicago Press, 1980), pp. 9–78.

2. For particularly useful ideas about the process of financial reform, see Thomas F. Cargill and Gillian G. Garcia, *Financial Reform in the 1980s* (Stanford, Calif.: Hoover Institution Press, 1985); Edward Kane, "Technological Regulatory Forces in the Developing Fusion of Financial-Services Competition," *Journal of Finance* 39 (July 1985), pp. 759–72; Thomas F. Huertas, "The Regulation of Financial Institutions: A Historical Perspective on Current Issues," in *Financial Services: The Changing Institutions and Government Policy.* The American Assembly (Englewood Cliffs, N.J.: Prentice-Hall, 1983); and Lewis J. Spellman, *The Depository Firm and Industry: Theory, History and Regulation* (New York: Academic Press, 1982).

3. Howard H. Hackley, "Our Baffling Banking System," *Virginia Law Review,* vol. 52, no. 4 (May 1966), p. 169.

4. Spellman, *The Depository Firm,* p. 23.

5. Huertas, "Regulation of Financial Institutions," pp. 13–14.

6. Of the commercial banks, 7,500 operated with national charters. See William J. Brown, "The Dual Banking System in the United States" (New York: American Bankers Association, 1976); U.S. Congress, Senate Committee on Banking, Housing, and Urban Affairs, Subcommittee on Financial Institutions, *Compendium of Issues Relating to Branching by Financial Institutions,* 94th Cong., 2nd sess., October 1976, Committee Print, p. 256; and Spellman, *The Depository Firm,* pp. 19–21, 228.

7. Samuel L. Hayes, et al., *Competition in the Investment Banking Industry* (Cambridge, Mass.: Harvard University Press, 1983), pp. 6–16.

8. Vincent Carosso, *Investment Banking in America: A History* (Cambridge, Mass.: Harvard University Press, 1970), chapters 2–4.

9. In 1869, the Supreme Court ruled (in *Paul v. Virginia*) that insurance was not interstate commerce and thus not susceptible to federal regulation, including antitrust policy; Emmett J. Vaughan, *Fundamentals of Risk and Insurance* (New York: John Wiley & Sons, 1982), p. 141.

10. H. Roger Grant, *Insurance Reform: Consumer Action in the Progressive Era* (Ames: University of Iowa Press, 1979), pp. 21–35.

11. Clay Herrick, *Trust Companies: Their Organization, Growth and Management* (New York: Bankers Publishing Company, 1915), pp. 12–32.

12. Edwin J. Perkins, "The Divorce of Commercial and Investment Banking: A History," *The Banking Law Journal,* vol. 88, no. 6 (June 1971), pp. 487–88.

13. Grant, *Insurance Reform,* pp. 37–51.

14. Paul L. Joskow, "Cartels, Competition and Regulation in the Property-liability Insurance Industry," *Bell Journal of Economics* (Autumn 1973), p. 392.

15. For details of early banking reform, see Eugene N. White, *The Regulation and Reform of the American Banking System, 1900–1929* (Princeton: Princeton University Press, 1983), especially chapters 2 and 3.

16. Huertas, "Regulation of Financial Institutions," p. 17.

17. Carosso, *Investment Banking in America*, chapter 6.

18. U.S. Congress, House Committee on Banking, *Report of the Committee to Investigate the Concentration of Money and Credit*, 62nd Cong., 3rd sess., 1913, p. 152.

19. Federal Reserve Act, 38 *Stat.* 251 (1913).

20. Assets of life insurance companies grew from $4.71 billion in 1914 to $18.03 billion in 1930; see, Elmer Hartzel, "Time Deposits," *Harvard Business Review* XII (October 1934), p. 36.

21. George W. Edwards, "Control of the Security-Investment System," *Harvard Business Review* XII (October 1933), pp. 6–7; Terris Moore, "Security Affiliate Versus Private Investment Banker—A Study in Security Originations," *Harvard Business Review* XII (July 1934), pp. 480–82.

22. U.S. Department of the Treasury, *Geographic Restrictions on Commercial Banking in the United States* (Washington, D.C.: GPO, 1981), p. 183.

23. *First National Bank in St. Louis v. Missouri*, 263 U.S. 640 (1924).

24. Quoted in Gerald C. Fischer and Carter H. Golembe, "The Branch Banking Provisions of the McFadden Act as Amended: Their Rationale and Rationality," in Senate Banking Committee, *Compendium on Branching*, pp. 1–42.

25. Office of the Comptroller of the Currency, *Annual Report for 1920*, vol. I, pp. 55–56.

26. Steven Osterweis, "Securities Affiliates and Security Operations of Commercial Banks," *Harvard Business Review* XI (October 1932), p. 126.

27. Quoted in Perkins, "The Divorce of Commercial and Investment Banking," p. 495.

28. For elaboration of this theme, see Harold van B. Cleveland and Thomas F. Huertas, *Citibank, 1812–1970* (Cambridge, Mass.: Harvard University Press, 1985), especially chapters 7 and 8; and Eugene N. White, "Banking Innovation in the 1920s: The Growth of National Banks' Financial Services," *Business and Economic History* 13 (1984), pp. 92–104.

29. Nelson W. Peach, *The Security Affiliates of National Banks* (Baltimore: n.p., 1941), p. 110.

30. Perkins, "The Divorce of Commercial and Investment Banking," p. 496.

31. Carosso, *Investment Banking*, pp. 285–88.

32. Descriptions of these proceedings can be found in Susan E. Kennedy, *The Banking Crisis of 1933* (Lexington: University of Kentucky Press, 1973), pp. 103–28; and Carosso, *Investment Banking*, pp. 323–51. The hearings themselves appear in the following: U.S. Congress, Senate Committee on Banking and Currency, *Stock Exchange Practices*, parts 5 and 6, 72nd Cong., 2nd sess., January–February 1933, and *Stock Exchange Practices*, parts 1–8, 73rd Cong., 1st sess., February–April 1933.

33. See Arthur M. Schlesinger, Jr., *The Crisis of the Old Order* (Boston: Houghton Mifflin, 1957), pp. 442–85; also, Ellis W. Hawley, *The New Deal and the Problem of Monopoly* (Princeton, N.J.: Princeton University Press, 1966), pp. 36–46.

34. Melanie Fein, "The Fragmented Depository Institutions System: A Case for Unification," *The American University Law Review*, vol. 29, no. 4 (Summer 1980), p. 664, n. 188.

35. Perkins, "Divorce of Commercial and Investment Banking," pp. 497–505.

36. H. Willis Parker and John M. Chapman, *The Banking Situation* (New York: Columbia University Press, 1934), pp. 62–83.

37. U.S. Congress, Senate Committee on Banking and Currency, *Stock Exchange Practices*, 73rd Cong., 2nd sess., June 1934, S. Rept. 1455, p. 155. Despite these views and the catalogue of abuses revealed in the Pecora hearings, and the consensus among reformers, empirical studies suggest that securities affiliates had little to do with the origins of the Great Depression or with undue risk to depositors; see Eugene N. White, "Before the Glass-Steagall Act: An Analysis of the Investment Banking Activities of National Banks." Working paper, Rutgers University, 1985.

38. Pub. L. 66, 48 *Stat.* 162 (1933), Secs. 5, 16, 20, 21, 32.

39. Parker and Chapman, *The Banking Situation*, pp. 99–100.

40. The bill had even provided for interstate branching within contiguous commercial areas; Fischer and Golembe, "Branch Banking," p. 31.

41. Federal Reserve Act, 48 *Stat.* 162 (1933), Secs. 8 and 23.

42. See Gerald Fischer, *Bank Holding Companies* (New York: Columbia University Press, 1961); and Donald T. Savage, "A History of the Bank Holding Company Movement, 1900–1978," in the Board of Governors of the Federal Reserve System, *The Bank Holding Company Movement to 1978: A Compendium* (Washington, D.C.: 1978), pp. 21–68.

43. Albert H. Cox, Jr., *Regulation of Interest Rates on Bank Deposits* (Ann Arbor: University of Michigan, 1966); also, Charles F. Haywood and Charles M. Linke, *The Regulation of Deposit Interest Rates* (Chicago: Association of Reserve City Bankers, 1968).

44. *Congressional Record* 3729, May 19, 1933.

45. Banking Act of 1935, Section 101 (g). See Herman Krooss, ed., *Documentary History of Banking and Currency in the United States* (New York: McGraw-Hill, 1969), vol. IV, p. 2890; also, Sam Peltzman, "Bank Entry Regulation: Its Impact and Purpose," *The National Banking Review* (December 1965), reprinted in Comptroller of the Currency, *Studies in Banking Competition and the Banking Structure* (Washington, D.C.: 1966), pp. 285–302.

46. Thomas McCraw, *Prophets of Regulation* (Cambridge, Mass.: Harvard University Press, 1984), pp. 162–76.

47. Louis Loss, *Securities Regulation* (Boston: Little, Brown, 1961), vol. I, pp. 23–64.

48. Pub. L. 73-22, 48 *Stat.* 74, in Federal Bar Association, *Federal Securities Laws, Legislative History*, vol. I, pp. 1–19.

49. McCraw, *Prophets of Regulation*, pp. 172–76.

50. Quoted in Carosso, *Investment Banking*, p. 362.

51. U.S. Congress, Senate, 73rd Cong., 2nd sess., 1934, S. Rept. 1455, p. 81.

52. U.S. Congress, House, 73rd Cong., 2nd sess., 1934, H. Rept. 1383, p. 15.

53. U.S. Congress, House Committee on Interstate and Foreign Commerce, *Hearings on H.R. 7852 and H.R. 8720*, 73rd Cong., 1st sess., 1934, p. 513.

54. McCraw, *Prophets of Regulation*, pp. 177–81.

55. *Congressional Record* 2268, February 9, 1934.

56. U.S. Congress, Senate Committee on Banking and Currency, *Hearings on S. Res. 84*, 73rd Cong., 2nd sess., 1934, pp. 6638–39.

57. Loss, *Securities Regulation*, vol. I, pp. 130–31.

58. McCraw, *Prophets of Regulation*, pp. 188–200.

59. Quoted from, "The Securities Markets: Findings and Recommendations of a Special Staff of the Twentieth Century Fund." U.S. Congress, Senate Committee on Banking, Subcommittee on Securities, *Securities Industry Study*, 93rd Cong., 1st sess., April 1973, S. Rept. 93-13, p. 143.

60. *Congressional Record* 2844, March 14, 1940.

61. This report, issued in five parts by the Securities and Exchange Commission, was entitled: *Report on the Study of Investment Trusts and Investment Companies*. Between the years 1938 and 1941, each part appeared as a House Document in the year of its completion.

62. Loss, *Securities Regulation*, vol. I, pp. 144–53.

63. *United States v. South-Eastern Underwriters Association*, 322 U.S. 533 (1944).

64. See, for example: U.S. Congress, House Committee on the Judiciary, 79th Cong., 1st sess., 1940, H. Rept. 143.

65. U.S. Department of Justice, Task Group on Antitrust Immunities, *The Pricing and Marketing of Insurance* (Washington, D.C.: January 1977), pp. 15–23.

66. Friedman, "Postwar Changes in American Financial Markets," p. 10.

67. Even before 1930 about 2 percent of all banks (although a small portion of their assets) failed annually—the average was 642, rising to 1,700 in the early 30s; see Parker and Chapman, *The Banking Situation*, p. 298.

68. See, for example, Bernard Shull and Paul M. Horvitz, "Branch Banking and the Structure of Competition" and "The Impact of Branch Banking on Bank Performance," in *Studies in Banking Competition*, pp. 99–186.

69. The number of bank holding companies declined from 52 in 1936 (with 14 percent of commercial bank deposits) to 48 in 1965 (8.3 percent of deposits); see Savage, "A History of the Bank Holding Company Movement," pp. 30, 50. Concentration ratios likewise declined, from 56.7 percent of deposits for the 100 largest banks in 1934 to 49.3 percent in 1966 (for the ten largest banks, the decline was from 23.7 percent to 20 percent); see Cynthia Glassman and Robert Eisenbeis, "Bank Holding Companies and Concentration of Banking and Financial Resources," in The Board of Governors of the Federal Reserve System, *The Banking Holding Company Movement to 1978: A Compendium* (Washington, D.C., 1978), p. 246.

70. 70 *Stat.* 133 (1956), Sec. 4 (c) (6).

71. In *United States v. The Philadelphia National Bank et al.*, 374 U.S. 321 (1963), the court enjoined a merger of PNB and Girard Trust, the second and third largest banks in Philadelphia, ruling that it would violate Section 7 of the Clayton Act—this, despite the approval of the merger by the Federal Reserve Board.

72. See Carosso, *Investment Banking*, pp. 480–81; and Hayes, et al., *Competition in the Investment Banking Industry*, pp. 118–19.

73. The Exchange Act provides no explicit antitrust exemption for organized exchanges (although the Maloney Act did so for the NASD). In the case of minimum rates, however, Section 19(a) of the act clearly grants the SEC authority to set brokerage commissions; see Loss, "Exchange Commission Rates and Impact of the Antitrust Laws on SEC Statutes Generally," in *Securities Regulation*, vol. V (supplement), pp. 3153–86.

74. U.S. Congress, Senate Committee on Banking, *Securities Industry Study*, pp. 137–239.

75. Since 1965 the number of holding companies has grown from 53 (multibank) companies with 8.3 percent of all commercial bank deposits to 5,409 (including one-bank companies) with 84 percent of all commercial bank deposits; see the Board of Governors of the Federal Reserve System, *Purposes & Functions* (Washington, D.C.: FRB, 1984), p. 95.

76. See Huertas, "Regulation of Financial Institutions," p. 23. For similar models of this self-adjusting tension, see Richard Vietor, *Energy Policy in America Since 1945* (New York: Cambridge University Press, 1984), pp. 1–12; and Edward J. Kane, "Accelerating Inflation, Technological Innovation, and the Decreasing Effectiveness of Banking Regulation," *Journal of Finance* 36 (May 1981), pp. 355–67.

77. Spellman uses this term to describe the windfall income that a bank receives from the depressed deposit costs due to Regulation Q; see Spellman, *The Depository Firm and Industry*, pp. 148–51.

78. Cox, *Regulation of Interest Rates*, p. 121.

79. Haywood and Linke, *Regulation of Deposit Interest Rates*, pp. 38–41; and Spellman, *The Depository Firm and Industry*, pp. 141–42.

80. Between 1960 and 1965, the yield on corporate bonds (Baa) had actually declined a bit, from 5.25 percent to 5.00 percent; during the next five years, it increased to 9.00 percent; see Herbert Dougall and Jack Gaumnitz, *Capital Markets and Institutions*, 3rd ed. (Englewood Cliffs, N.J.: Prentice-Hall, 1975), p. 173.

81. New public bond issues, which had been growing at about 3 percent (1960–1965) accelerated to 35 percent (1965–1970); new equity issues also accelerated, but the amount was relatively small when compared to bonds. Ibid., pp. 169, 180.

82. These and other private innovations are discussed in Cargill and Garcia, *Financial Reform*, chapter 7.

83. Savage, "A History of the Bank Holding Company Movement," pp. 56, 62–65.

84. Office of Technology Assessment, *Effects of Information Technology on Financial Service Systems* (Washington, D.C.: 1984), especially chapters 3 and 4; Alan Gart, *Banks, Thrifts, & Insurance Companies* (Lexington, Mass.: D. C. Heath Company, 1985), pp. 11–50; and Susan Ingram, "Recent Developments in Electronic Banking," *The Bankers Magazine* (July–August 1985), pp. 50–59.

85. And to this, Kane notes the perverse opportunity to cross-subsidize nondepository financial products with the spillover benefits of deposit insurance; see Kane, "Technological Regulatory Forces," p. 763.

86. In addition to these geographic effects, EFT has a variety of implications for monetary policy: definition of monetary aggregates and targets, velocity, and secondary linkages between money supply and real sector variables (i.e., prices and income). See, for example, Elinor H. Solomon, "EFT and the Money Supply," *The Bankers Magazine* (July–August, 1985), pp. 77–81; also, Cargill and Garcia, *Financial Reform*, pp. 99–140.

87. On Glass-Steagall in particular, see White, "Before the Glass-Steagall Act," (note 37 supra); Golembe Associates, *Commercial Banking and the Glass-Steagall Act* (Washington, D.C.: American Bankers Association, 1982); J. P. Morgan & Co., "Rethinking Glass-Steagall" (New York, December 1984); and U.S. Congress, Senate Committee on Banking, Subcommittee on Securities, *Securities Activities of Depository Institutions*, 97th Cong., 2nd sess., February 1982. Concerning the causes of the Great Depression in general, the fundamental reassessment that monetary policy (and not banking or speculation) was the problem came from Milton Friedman and Anna Schwartz, *A Monetary History of the United States, 1867–1960* (Princeton, N.J.: Princeton University Press, 1963); see also Clark Warburton, *Depression, Inflation, and Monetary Policy: Selected Papers, 1945–1953* (Baltimore: Johns Hopkins University Press, 1966).

88. See, for example, George J. Benston, "Interest Payments on Demand Deposits and Bank Investment Behavior," *Journal of Political Economy* 72 (October 1964), pp. 431–39; Alfred Kahn, *Economics of Regulation: Principles and Institutions* (New York: John Wiley & Sons, 1971), vol. II, chapter 5 ("Destructive Competition and the Quality of Service," especially pp. 193–209); State of New York, Insurance Department, *Cartels vs. Competition: A Critique of Insurance Price Regulation* (New York, 1975); and Joskow, "Cartels, Competition, and Regulation," (see note 14 supra).

89. See U.S. Congress, Senate Committee on Banking, Subcommittee on Financial Institutions, *Compendium of Issues Relating to Branching by Financial Institutions*, 94th Cong., 2nd sess., October 1976, Committee Print—see especially the papers by Shull, Fischer and Davis, Talley, Benston, and Gilbert and Longbrake; Douglas Ginsburg, *Interstate Banking* (Cambridge, Mass.: Center for Information Policy Research, 1983); Robert A. Eisenbeis, *Financial Innovation and the Role of Regulation: Implications for Banking Organization, Structure and Regulations* (Washington, D.C.: The Board of Governors of the Federal Reserve System, 1980) and "Bank Holding Companies and Public Policy," in Benston, *Financial Services: Changing Institutions and Government Policy* (Englewood Cliffs, N.J.: Prentice-Hall, 1983), pp. 127–55; and Stephen A. Rhoades, *Mergers and Acquisitions by Commercial Banks, 1960–83*, Staff Studies No. 142 (Washington, D.C.: The Board of Governors of the Federal Reserve System, January 1985).

90. In addition to an amazing number of congressional hearings, a series of blue-ribbon studies framed the public policy issues. For example, in 1971 the Hunt Commission (named after its chairman, Reed O. Hunt) issued the *Report of the President's Commission on Financial Structure and Regulation*; in 1973 the Senate Committee on Banking published the *Securities Industry Study* (see note 59 supra); in 1975, the House of Representatives produced the FINE report—U.S. Congress, House Committee on Banking, Currency and Housing, *The Financial Institutions and the Nation's Economy*, 94th Cong., 1st sess., 1975; in 1980 the Treasury Department published the *Report of the Interagency Task Force on Thrift Institutions* (Washington, D.C.: June 1980); and in 1984 the Task Group on Regulation of Financial Services issued *Blueprint for Reform* (Washington, D.C.: July 1984).

91. For an analysis of deregulation (in other sectors than financial services) that attributes causation primarily to new ideas, see Martha Derthick and Paul J. Quirk, *The Politics of Deregulation* (Washington, D.C.: The Brookings Institution, 1985), especially pp. 29–57.

92. National Association of Insurance Commissioners, Staff Study, "Monitoring Competition: A Means of Regulating the Property and Liability Insurance Business" (1974), p. 65.

93. Justice Department, *Pricing and Marketing of Insurance*, p. 29.

94. Joskow, "Cartels, Competition, and Regulation," pp. 406–07, 417–18.

95. William Baumol, John Panzar, and Robert Willig, *Contestable Markets and the Theory of Industry Structure* (New York: Harcourt Brace Jovanovich, 1982).

96. State of New York, Insurance Department, *Cartels vs. Competition*, pp. 13–19, 70–73.

97. U.S. Congress, House Committee on the Judiciary, Subcommittee on Monopolies and Commercial Law, *Competition in the Insurance Industry*, 98th Cong., 2nd sess., April 1984, pp. 14–15.

98. Their share of the total volume increased from 24.3 percent to 42.4 percent (by 1970); their share of stock ownership grew from 17 percent to 25 percent; Ibid., p. 38.

99. Gregg A. Jarrell, "Change at the Exchange: The Causes and Effects of Deregulation," *Journal of Law and Economics* XXVII (October 1984), p. 277.

100. Joel Seligman, *The Transformation of Wall Street* (Boston: Houghton Mifflin, 1982), pp. 388–95.

101. U.S. Congress, Senate Committee on Banking, *Securities Industry Study*, pp. 68–71.

102. *Kaplan* v. *Lehman Bros.*, 250 F. Supp. 562 (1966), aff'd, 371 F. 2d 409 (1967), cert. denied, 389 U.S. 954 (1967).

103. Seligman, *Transformation of Wall Street*, pp. 397–403.

104. Quoted in Kahn, *Economics of Regulation*, II, p. 198, n. 76.

105. Securities and Exchange Commission, "Special Study of the Securities Markets." Published by U.S. Congress, House, 88th Cong., 1st sess., 1963, H. Doc. 95, p. 427.

106. U.S. Congress, Senate Committee on Banking, *Securities Industry Study*, 92nd Cong., 2nd sess., 1972, Committee Print, pp. 7–8.

107. U.S. Congress, Senate Committee on Banking, *Securities Industry Study*, p. 2; another influential study of the likely effects of deregulation was released in 1972 by Irwin Friend and Marshall Blume. In "The Consequences of Competitive Commissions on the New York Stock Exchange" (working paper: Wharton School, April 1972), Friend and Blume concluded that deregulation would have no negative effects, in aggregate, on the industry or its customers.

108. Securities and Exchange Commission, Directorate of Economic and Policy Analysis, *Survey of Commission Charges on Brokerage Transactions* (Washington, D.C.: 1981).

109. Steven D. Felgran, "Bank Entry into Securities Brokerage: Competitive and Legal Aspects," *New England Economic Review* (November 1984), pp. 12–33.

110. Haywood and Linke, *Regulation of Deposit Interest Rates*, pp. 41–43.

111. The average number of S&L offices, per association, increased from 1.48 in 1965 to 5.16 by 1981; this increase was much larger than the corresponding increase for commercial banks (from 2.15 to 3.74), which had a wider, less-regulated range of opportunity to expand liabilities; see Cargill and Garcia, *Financial Reform*, p. 93.

112. Andrew S. Carron, *The Plight of the Thrift Institutions* (Washington, D.C.: The Brookings Institution, 1982), chapter 1; also, Cargill and Garcia, *Financial Reform*, pp. 76–81.

113. Ibid., pp. 57–60.

114. Edward J. Kane, *The Gathering Crisis in Federal Deposit Insurance* (Cambridge, Mass.: MIT Press, 1985), pp. 70–71.

115. Kenneth Spong, *Banking Regulation: Its Purposes, Implementation, and Effects* (Kansas City: Federal Reserve Bank of Kansas City, 1983), pp. 100–101; also, Lawrence J. White,

"The Partial Deregulation of Banks and Other Depository Institutions," in *Regulatory Reform: What Actually Happened*, Leonard W. Weiss and Michael W. Klass, eds. (Boston: Little, Brown, 1985), pp. 169–209.

116. Salomon Brothers, Inc., *Stock Research, Commercial Banks*, November 29 and December 17, 1985.

117. *The Wall Street Journal*, June 11, 1985.

118. Quoted in Stephen Koepp, "Banking Takes a Beating," *Time*, December 3, 1984, p. 50.

119. For detailed discussion of this issue, see Dekkers L. Davidson and Richard Vietor, *The Comptroller and Nonbank Banks*, Case no. 0-385-248 (Boston: Harvard Business School, Case Services, 1984); also, Arthur E. Wilmarth, Jr., "The Federal Reserve Board's Nonbank Bank Dilemma," in *Bank Structure and Competition* (Chicago: Federal Reserve Bank of Chicago, 1984), pp. 231–48.

120. 12 U.S.C. s.1841(c).

121. Federal Reserve Bank of Chicago, "What is a Bank?" *Economic Perspectives* (January 1983), pp. 20, 24.

122. U.S. Congress, House, 84th Cong., 1st sess., 1955, H. Rept. 84, p. 609.

123. Davidson and Vietor, *The Comptroller and Nonbank Banks*, p. 10.

124. U.S. Congress, Senate Committee on Banking, Housing, and Urban Affairs, *Competitive Equity in the Financial Services Industry*, 98th Cong., 2nd sess., March 1984, pp. 1221–28, 1274–87, 1583–92.

125. Press release, Conference of State Bank Supervisors to Congress, February 22, 1985, p. 2.

126. *The Wall Street Journal*, January 22, 1986.

127. Harvey Rosenblum, "Banks and Nonbanks: Who's in Control?" *The Bankers Magazine* (September–October, 1984), p. 13.

THREE

BREAKING RELATIONSHIPS:
THE ADVENT OF PRICE BANKING
IN THE UNITED STATES

David M. Meerschwam

In the United States a shift from relationship to price banking has taken place as price-driven financial instruments have become increasingly important. Especially during the late 1970s, the transition from relationship to price banking resulted in considerable financial deregulation, but the development of price-driven financial instruments had begun much earlier. In this chapter, the product innovation and institutional change that have characterized the financial system of the United States are treated as the most important manifestations of this shift toward price banking. As a result of this shift, the stability of the financial system has once again become a topic of major concern because bank failures have reemerged as issues of practical relevance and are no longer of only theoretical interest. Although the stability of the financial system is hardly a new concern, it has recently attracted renewed attention. In this chapter, I consider the emergence of price banking and the parallel decline of relationship banking as requisites to understanding the contemporary American financial environment. I concentrate on developments in the banking world, but the increased emphasis on prices can be seen throughout the financial industry.

INTRODUCTION

The term *relationship banking* is used in this chapter to refer to a banking environment in which financial transactions are seen as part of a continuing and unfolding relationship between fi-

This chapter greatly benefited from discussions with M. Colyer Crum. Many of the ideas expressed here reflect our joint work as presented in M. C. Crum and D. M. Meerschwam, "From Relationship to Price Banking: The Loss of Regulatory Control," in *America vs. Japan*, ed. T. K. McCraw (Boston, Mass.: Harvard Business School Press, 1986). Errors and omissions remain, of course, my own responsibility.

nancial intermediaries and their customers. *Price banking*, on the other hand, describes financial transactions that are seen as independent, price-driven events; current prices and terms determine the current allocation of funds as they are placed with the highest bidder, and many similar financial instruments compete through prices. In this latter environment it is more likely that funds are moved to another financial partner when prices are attractive, since each transaction is seen as an independent event.

This does not mean that prices play no role in relationship banking. What matters in a relationship environment is that current prices are not sufficient to (and are not usually allowed to) determine the allocation of funds. Thus it is possible for a particular transaction to take place at a price and on terms that do not purely reflect current market conditions; instead, the arrangement also takes into consideration the value of possible future interactions between the partners in the financial transaction. More formally, the transaction can be viewed as an intertemporal optimization problem that is characterized by price restrictions and high information costs. In such relationship environments, frequent and rapid partner changes between lenders, financial intermediaries, and borrowers are less likely than they are in a price-driven environment where the actors primarily follow price signals that fluctuate more freely and therefore carry more information. In a relationship system, then, the ability to attract and gain access to funds is partly vested in the relationship itself. The development and maintenance of these relationships in the United States provided long-term banking stability.

The emergence of a relationship system in the United States was the outcome of a long historical process, and the dramatic changes that took place in the U.S. banking industry during the first half of the 1980s have deep roots in earlier developments. In fact, these recent events can be understood only when we recognize that from the earliest days of the American republic public fear of powerful central financial institutions helped shape our financial environment and its institutional arrangements. By 1970 approximately 50,000 institutions coexisted in a highly segmented financial market. Not only was the product market segmented, but numerous geographical restrictions were also in place. Interstate branch banking was prohibited, and banks had to observe specific restrictions imposed by state legislatures. Furthermore, the prices of many products offered by the financial intermediaries were regulated, and limitations on loan size, relative to bank capital, placed further restrictions on lending activities. This segmentation and price regulation sharply curtailed the freedom of players in the market; financial institutions could compete only with a limited number of products, while customers faced limited opportunities. American banking was a relatively simple industry; in funding, well-defined products were sold under price ceilings, and in lending, long-standing customers were the target.

As interest rates rose during the middle 1960s and 1970s, changes occurred; relationships lost in value because price-oriented instruments, developed by financial innovators, tried to exploit newly identified market opportunities. The traditional fundamentals that had allowed for, and even encouraged, the development of relationships were increasingly compromised as the emerging influence of price banking gave financial institutions more and more opportunities to buy and sell money. In this environment, funding transactions could easily be entered into through price competition without having to rely on carefully developed relationships. Money increasingly depended on prices.

Seeming to ignore this trend, regulatory agencies did not adjust their policies, and financial institutions increasingly escaped regulation as they moved toward price banking. Thus by the middle 1980s, when several banks got into serious liquidity trouble, the traditional safety nets seemed both insufficient and ill-suited to the new circumstances. In this chapter, I first present an historical sketch that illustrates how a highly fragmented system developed in the United States and then I describe the evolution in institutional arrangements that has fostered the development of price banking. For purposes of illustration I have primarily focused on commercial banking, with the understanding that the transition from relationship to price banking represents a pervasive trend throughout the contemporary financial services industry.

An element of speculation underlies the interpretation provided here. This should not be surprising; it is inherent in the

nature of the banking industry that "proofs" are difficult to document because once one goes beyond pure description, one en-
counters the issue of confidence—the most central and most
intangible aspect of banking. It is this confidence that forms the
basis of a stable system. Therefore, my presentation is selective;
it ignores many recent changes in order to concentrate on the
larger forces of secular change that have allowed financial institutions to operate differently and more freely. Before evaluating the recent environment, however, the early development of
the financial system and the way in which fragmentation nurtured relationships will be reviewed.

EARLY BANKING IN THE UNITED STATES (1776–1933)

From the beginning, banking in the United States depended
on carefully developed relationships because financing arrangements had to develop around small, individual banks. A federal
charter was granted to the National Bank of the United States
only after much debate, and state legislatures remained a barrier to interstate branch banking; in this environment, correspondent banking flourished. The rudimentary communication
and transportation systems also contributed to the development
of a highly fragmented banking system. In any particular geographical area, repeated transactions between a bank and its
customers became likely since a continuing relationship reduced
information costs; the relationship functioned as a signal about
the quality of both the customer and the intermediary. Thus,
fragmentation in the financial system contributed to the development of relationships.[1]

Early American banking was characterized by the trade-off
between, on the one hand, the nation's desire to decentralize
banking (because of fear of powerful, central, financial institutions) and, on the other hand, the potential instability associated with the risk represented by many small independent
banks, each one susceptible to liquidity problems.[2] There are
many illustrations of this trade-off, such as the failure to recharter the Second National Bank of the United States in 1836. The
Second National Bank, like its predecessor, only came into be-

ing after a lengthy debate that weighed the costs and advantages of centralization. Although the Second National Bank had functioned well, opponents of a strong, federally chartered bank argued that such an institution was dangerous and unconstitutional.[3] In a hearing during the recharter debate, the Second National Bank's president attempted to dispel the fears by arguing that the bank had acted responsibly and that no state bank had ever been injured by it, even though, as he noted, "[T]here are very few banks which might not have been destroyed by an exertion of the power of the Bank."[4] His statement, intended to show the careful exercise of the bank's responsibility, unintentionally highlighted its latent power. This shadowy power persuaded Congress not to renew the charter of the country's only national bank. As a result, only state banks were permitted to operate after 1836, and fragmentation of the American banking system seemed well assured.

Almost thirty years later, wartime financial difficulties forced the passage of the National Banking Act of 1863, which firmly established a dual character in the U.S. banking system by permitting nationally chartered banks.[5] Thereafter, national and state banks coexisted; they offered similar products, even though a tax law had made it impossible for the state banks to issue notes.[6] The 1863 act guaranteed that there was competition even at the regulatory level since banks could choose between state and national charters. But even after the act institutionalized the dual system, threats to decentralization continued to appear.

One such threat provides a second illustration of the trade-off between the fears of centralization and risks of decentralization—the development of "trusts" during the late nineteenth century. At that time, a group of financial institutions that developed around J. P. Morgan offered financial services as diverse as insurance, and commercial and trust banking. Banks such as New York's First National and National City also moved toward what is now called "universal banking." But as the power of a few banks grew, traditional suspicions against all banking power became stronger. In 1912 the Pujo committee investigated the "money trusts" and unambiguously denounced them. It charged the existence of

> . . . a community of interests between a few leaders of finance, created and held together through stock ownership, interlocking directorates, partnership and joint account transactions, and other forms of domination over banks, trust companies, railroads and public service and industrial corporations, which has resulted in great and rapidly growing concentration of the control of money and credit in the hands of these few men.[7]

By 1914 many of these interrelationships had been broken and the perceived threat posed by dominant banks soon abated. The other side of the trade-off, however—small bank instability—had already reappeared. After a demonstration of the weaknesses of decentralized banking in the banking panic of 1907, a 1908 act commissioned the extensive study of foreign financial systems.[8] The study recommended a central (government) bank for the United States. But this proposal appeared at the height of the debate following the Pujo committee's deliberations, when the public mood had again turned against centralized banking, and the recommendation for a central bank was turned down.

Yet the need for some central institution to foster banking stability remained; and it was answered by the Federal Reserve Act of 1913. Although that act did not establish a powerful central bank for the United States, it did create an unusual institution—the Federal Reserve System—that represented yet another example of the nation's abiding fear of centralized financial powers. As a compromise born of the trade-off between stability and decentralization, the Federal Reserve System was both fragmented (by virtue of its twelve district Federal Reserve Banks) and centralized (through its central unit, the relatively weak Federal Reserve Board).[9] The two primary objectives of the new system were to create an elastic supply of currency and to supervise the national financial system. While state regulators controlled state banks, the Comptroller of the Currency and the Federal Reserve System supervised national banking. Even though this dual banking system seemed to guarantee diversity, a large number of relatively small, individual banks often found it difficult to establish the credibility and the quality leadership required to function smoothly in an industry where confidence was of prime importance. As in the past, the price of decentralization was some compromise of stability.

In fact, by the early 1930s, instability in the financial system had again become a major public issue; fragmentation had assured diffusion of power, but at a cost. Although the Federal Reserve System existed, its powers were too small, its experience too limited, and its tools too restricted to impose stability on a volatile system.[10] When Franklin D. Roosevelt became president, the banking crisis was at its height, and new banking legislation became a top priority. In 1933, a new banking act was passed that, in order to protect investors and to assure diversity, carefully segmented commercial from investment banking. Furthermore, to enhance stability of the financial system, the power of the Federal Reserve System was strengthened, and a Federal Deposit Insurance Corporation was established to safeguard small depositors and to stop frequent runs on banks.

The Federal Deposit Insurance Corporation (FDIC), represented the third federal regulatory agency authorized to oversee commercial banks. The National Banking Act of 1863 established the Comptroller of the Currency to charter, supervise, and examine national banks. The Federal Reserve Act of 1913 set up the Federal Reserve System to supervise all member banks (i.e., all national banks and all state banks that elected to join the system). The Banking Act of 1933 created the FDIC, which regulated all banks that purchased the insurance it offered. Federal Reserve banks were required to do so; others could elect to apply for membership. It is striking that even in the new climate of regulation great diversity was achieved. Multiple regulators functioned on the national level, and banks could still opt to be supervised by the state authorities provided they were willing to forego membership in the Federal Reserve System and in the FDIC.

Segmentation and regulation therefore provided the two key characteristics of the financial system in the United States; geographical and product market segmentation restricted the alternatives available to capital suppliers, users, and their intermediaries in carrying out financial transactions, and the prices charged for these transactions were often regulated. Fixed brokerage rates, first set by a cartel in 1792, were reaffirmed by the Securities Exchange Act of 1934. Regulation Q, in effect since

1933, set maximum rates for various types of deposit and savings accounts. Savings and loan institutions also faced price restrictions after 1966, when Regulation Q was extended to cover these institutions.[11] In short, regulation of many segments of the financial industry was broad, deep, and carefully administered.

The following paragraphs discuss how this fragmentation limited financing alternatives and put relationships at the center of the system. What must be stressed here is that the systematic reduction in alternatives *within* a particular product or geographical area led to a large number of independent institutions nationwide. Because of market segmentation, these institutions were not in direct competition with each other. Consolidation took place only when financial products could *not* be geographically segmented; for example, a small number of major investment banks in New York City emerged to service the national securities underwriting market.

YEARS OF STABILITY (1934–1980)

Whereas between 1929 and 1933 over 9,056 banks failed (putting the total since 1921 at over 14,000), the years that followed were characterized by great stability.[12] Bank failure became an infrequent phenomenon. Each year between 1945 and 1980 an average of only about 6 banks closed because of financial difficulty.[13] At a glance, the system that operated after the Second World War seemed to have offered (remarkably) both diversity and stability. A closer look shows that it was regulated diversity, through sharp differentiation along product and geographical lines, that enhanced financial stability in what was a generally prosperous and stable economic environment.[14]

Long-lasting relationships developed because the cost of switching financial partners, due to both limited alternatives and the lack of price competition, was high. In switching from one financial institution to another, a borrower had to reestablish his credentials as the information vested in an existing relationship was lost and the accumulated, mutual, noncontractual obligations were dissipated. For the financial institutions themselves, it was important to persuade depositors that the cost of turning to another banking institution was high. Given price and product restrictions, savers gained little by switching, and banks depended on the reliable access to funds provided by relationships that tied customers to a particular institution. Taken together, the importance for the stability of the financial system of increased switching costs and reduced information costs for the ongoing associations can hardly be exaggerated.

One good example of "relationship money" can be seen in the funds made available through demand deposit accounts to commercial banks. Since rates offered on time deposits were regulated, and demand deposits could offer no interest at all, there was little incentive for the depositor to switch banks. Banks were left to compete through services and conveniences, and this fostered ongoing relationships. Furthermore, stable sources of low-cost funds and the regulatory-created difficulties that reduced funding alternatives made the rapid growth of assets unlikely and moderated the return requirements on the asset side of the bank's balance sheet. This in turn allowed for conservative asset management and further enhanced the stability of the banking sector. Table 3-1 shows the asset and liability composition of commercial banks. The importance of demand deposits in funding is clear; in 1950, for example, demand deposits stood at 70 percent of total assets.

But it was not only a lack of price competition that enhanced banking relationships; fragmentation of the system, caused by regulated product differentiation, fostered many different types of institutions to service distinct parts of the market. Commercial banks, savings and loans, mutual savings banks, credit unions, life insurance companies, private, state, and local pension funds, finance companies, open-ended investment companies, securities dealers and brokers, real estate investment trusts, and money market funds all competed in differentiated product areas, and each maintained its own set of relationships. Table 3-2 shows the size of these institutions by asset holdings.

In terms of total assets, commercial banks comprised the largest single group. While they offered the most diversified product line, they were nonetheless considerably restricted. In deposit taking, for example, branching restrictions (on local banks) and price regulation defined markets. In these markets, some substitutability did exist where savings and loans operated side by side with the commercial banks; yet these thrift institutions could

Table 3-1
Selected Assets and Liabilities of Commercial Banks
($ billion)

	1950	1955	1960	1965	1970	1975	1980	1984
Assets								
U.S. government securities	63.9	64.5	63.2	65.3	75.7	119.0	172.1	259.4
State and local obligations	8.1	12.7	17.6	38.7	69.6	102.0	149.2	175.0
Consumer credit	7.4	13.2	20.6	35.7	53.9	90.3	180.2	259.6
Bank loans N.E.C.	27.7	42.2	62.3	104.9	152.4	257.3	457.9	642.6
Total	148.2	185.0	225.1	336.4	490.7	822.3	1,389.5	2,019.1
Liabilities								
Demand deposits[a]	95.7	114.3	123.7	146.9	182.5	236.8	342.0	414.9
Time deposits	36.9	50.3	73.3	147.2	231.7	453.1	745.8	1,097.1
Total	137.7	171.4	206.9	312.8	459.4	775.1	1,309.4	1,873.7

[a]For 1980 and 1984, the figures represent checkable deposits.
Source: The Board of Governors of the Federal Reserve System, *Flow of Funds Accounts, 1946–1975*, and *Flow of Funds Accounts, 1961–1984*.

not offer many standard banking services, and they were restricted in lending. Legislation channeled the funds collected by these institutions to government securities and, through mortgage lending, to the housing markets.[15]

Short-term business loans were handled by the commercial banks. (Their name derives from their role in making such "commercial" loans.) For corporations, there were few real alternatives to the commercial banks' working capital loans; only later, during the 1970s, did other financing instruments such as commercial paper begin to play an important role in corporate finance for the strongest and largest borrowers.

Geographical segmentation restricted the number of feasible banking partners for all but the largest national corporations. While it was possible to do business with banks in other states, lack of convenient access effectively limited the choices for most corporations and stimulated local relationships. The largest corporations circumvented geographical segmentation; because of the size of their transactions, they could establish relationships with the largest banks, irrespective of location. Smaller banks were inadequate for these corporations because of the legal limits on their lending relative to bank capital. Traditionally, the largest

Table 3-2
Relative Size of Selected Financial Institutions
(assets as a percentage of industry total)

	1950	1955	1960	1965	1970	1975	1980	1984
Depository Institutions								
Commercial banks	50.6	44.4	39.8	40.0	41.6	42.9	40.2	39.5
Savings and loans	6.2	9.6	13.3	15.9	15.4	17.9	18.2	18.7
Mutual savings banks	8.6	8.3	7.8	7.3	6.9	6.4	5.0	4.0
Credit unions	0.3	0.5	0.9	1.1	1.4	1.8	1.9	2.3
Total	65.7	62.8	61.8	64.4	65.3	69.0	65.2	64.5
Nondepository Institutions								
Life insurance companies	23.4	22.5	21.3	18.3	16.3	13.5	12.4	8.4
Private pension funds	2.1	3.1	4.0	3.9	3.4	2.9	5.9	6.8
State and local government retirement funds	1.9	2.9	3.8	4.2	4.6	4.5	4.8	5.5
Other insurance companies	2.9	3.2	3.1	2.7	3.0	3.1	4.0	3.3
Finance companies	3.3	4.7	5.2	5.7	5.8	5.4	6.0	6.3
Open-ended investment companies	0.1	0.2	0.4	0.5	0.7	0.4	0.5	1.8
Securities brokers and dealers	0.6	0.4	0.4	0.3	0.6	0.2	0.2	0.2
REIT's	0.0	0.0	0.0	0.0	0.4	0.8	0.1	0.1
Money market funds	0.0	0.0	0.0	0.0	0.0	0.1	0.8	3.2
Total	34.3	37.2	38.2	35.6	34.7	31.0	34.8	35.5
Total Assets of Identified Institutions ($ billion)	247.9	356.8	496.4	751.9	1,071.1	1,738.1	3,105.1	4,425.5

Source: The Board of Governors of the Federal Reserve System, *Flow of Funds Accounts, 1946–1975*, and *Flow of Funds Accounts, 1961–1984*.

share of bank loans went to short- and medium-term commercial and industrial (C&I) projects, at rates linked to the prime rate.[16] In fact, there were only a few alternatives (such as private placements by insurance companies) to commercial bank loans in short-term and intermediate-term finance; the commercial paper and bankers acceptances' markets had not yet attained their current importance, and the transactions that took place in those markets were unimportant compared to bank credit. For example, in 1960, total commercial paper outstanding was $3 billion; in 1970, it was $33 billion; and in 1980, the figure reached $130 billion. For bankers acceptances, comparable numbers were $1 billion in 1960, $7 billion in 1970, and $55 billion in 1980. Thus, for a considerable part of the post–World War II period, it remained important for corporations to have access to bank credit lines. An important way of assuring such access was to have a stable relationship with a bank.

In long-term finance, both equity and debt issues were, at least in theory, available to companies. In these markets, commercial banks could not offer their services as intermediaries. In placing debt or selling equity, prices played a more direct role. The equity market was never an important source of funds, and in the debt market, the benchmark rate (government bond interest) varied. But even in this market, given the benchmark rate, a particular firm's ability to access funds depended not only on the company's rating but also on its relationship with the securities firm that was to underwrite the new issue.[17]

Banks were also restricted in their own funding; they were barred from the growing accumulations of funds in several important potential markets. Both the life insurance and pension businesses remained closed to banks; and even in the markets that were open, Regulation Q restricted the rates that could be offered (see Table 3-3).

It is sometimes suggested that price regulation did not really matter, since the rates offered on the various accounts typically remained well below the ceilings set by Regulation Q. Thus, it is argued, if banks had been willing to compete for funds on a price basis, they could have done so. Given the geographically segmented nature of the market, however, the general availability of credit (in contrast to the credit crunches of the late 1960s),

Table 3-3
Regulation Q, January 31, 1979

Type of Deposit	Interest Rate Ceilings
Savings Deposits	4.50%
Other Time Deposits	
Multiple Maturity Deposits	
30–89 days	4.50
90–365 days	5.00
1–2 years	5.50
2 years or more	5.75
Single Maturity Deposits	
Less than $100,000	
30–365 days	5.00
1–2 years	5.50
2 years or more	5.75
$100,000 and over	
30–59 days	6.25
60–89 days	6.50
90–179 days	6.75
180–365 days	7.00
1 year or more	7.50

Source: Federal Reserve Bulletin.

and the limited profitability allowed by the regulators, price competition among banks for deposits seemed of only secondary importance. In addition, the interest rate constraints (zero percent) for demand deposits *were* binding, and this was of great importance. Not only did demand deposits stand at 60 percent of total assets in 1960, they often constituted the first transaction between a check-writing customer and a bank. Thus, the absence of price competition in the demand deposit market was crucially important in creating the relationship environment.

THE MOVE TO PRICE BANKING

In the stable post–World War II financial environment, the relationship system allowed financial intermediaries to make profits in a relatively simple and uninnovative environment: "It was as if a marathon race ended in a 15,000-way tie as almost all

15,000 commercial banks in the U.S. showed profits and hardly any failures occurred."[18] Yet after 1951, change began to occur when the Federal Reserve Board started to pursue a more independent policy, rather than cooperate closely with the Treasury.[19] During these postwar years, interest rates, as reflected in Treasury bill prices, showed a dramatic increase from less than 3 percent in the 1950s to more than 14 percent in the early 1980s (see Figure 3-1). As a result, the lure of price competition increased.

Yet, even where banks saw increasingly profitable lending opportunities, price regulation restricted their ability to compete for funds. At the same time, depositors became more and more aware of the opportunity cost of holding price-regulated instruments. As interest rates rose, the attractiveness of price-driven instruments increased. For those who supplied these funds, higher returns became available; for the intermediaries, the reward of innovative instruments lay in their ability to attract large pools of funds. At first the innovations were simple, the numbers few, and the sums involved small. But when the inflation of the late 1960s and the 1970s magnified interest rate fluctuations, price banking became more attractive to lenders, borrowers, and intermediaries in the U.S. financial markets; as the constraints on the products of the banks and other financial institutions crumbled, a massive shift developed in competitive emphasis from reliance on nurturing continuing relationships to an expanding emphasis on price competition both in the gathering and in the employment of funds.

It should be emphasized that although more and more arm's-length, rate-sensitive money became available to financial institutions in the early stages of this development, traditional relationship channels remained dominant, as only a few price instruments were available. Still, the introduction and growth of price money as an alternative to relationship money increasingly acted to change the entire character of the financial markets. Regulatory competition, the ambiguity of specific regulations, and concerns of regulators over the funding ability of banks, all encouraged the careful introduction of a few market-related alternatives to the stable relationship instruments discussed above.

Figure 3-1
U.S. *Interest Rates, 1945–1981*

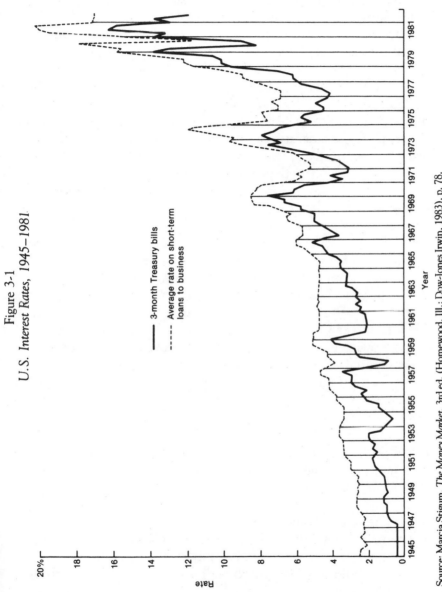

——— 3-month Treasury bills

- - - - - Average rate on short-term
loans to business

Source: Marcia Stigum, *The Money Market*, 3rd ed. (Homewood, Ill.: Dow-Jones Irwin, 1983), p. 78.

THE CD MARKET

One popular device to gather market funds without a stable relationship was the negotiable certificate of deposit (CD) (developed in 1961 by Citibank).[20] CD's were certificates that stated the size, maturity, and interest rate for a particular (large) deposit. The certificates carried the name of the deposit-taking institution, as well as the name of the depositor; many were traded actively in secondary markets, which Citibank worked to develop. In these markets, given the perceived quality of the issuer, price considerations were of primary importance. The CD was fundamentally different from the deposit made to an ordinary deposit account; depositors bought a CD as an independent event, looking simply for the most attractive interest rate of the moment. Typically the depositor was locked in for the term of the certificate, but for the largest CD's (as noted), the holder could choose either to keep it or sell it in the secondary market.

Although initial rates offered on the CD's were still subject to regulation, they were effectively determined by the quality of the name of the issuing institution and the overall availability of money. By 1969, Regulation Q, which had been extended in 1961 to cover CD rates, had become a binding constraint; by then, however, other alternatives to relationship money had been devised. Regulators, observing the substitution of other, price-determined instruments (especially Euromarket funds) for regulated CD's, freed the rates that could be offered on CD's in 1973.

The CD market also allowed banks to avoid the geographical restrictions that had determined their intake of stable relationship money through deposit accounts. In their massive study of the history of Citibank, two bank executives noted that

> [The CD] would solve the funding problem, thereby opening the way to faster growth. Instead of matching loan commitments to the supply of bonds that could be sold, banks would now be able to book loans they thought profitable, knowing the funds would be available in the market at a price. Moreover, market funding would solve another traditional banking problem: liquidity. If banks could find funds whenever needed in large, efficient CD and Eurodol-

lar markets, they would be able to shift their assets port-folios away from low-yielding but highly liquid U.S. government securities toward higher-yielding but less liquid assets such as loans and municipal securities.[21]

Thus, while banks became able to obtain money from different geographical areas, the type of available money was also fundamentally different from ordinary deposits. Large CD money proved much less stable since it moved quickly in response to price stimuli and liquidity or solvency problems. Furthermore, it was not insured through the FDIC, since the minimum size of the CD's exceeded the FDIC insurance maximum.

Yet the new instruments proved popular. In 1965, $10 billion of domestic CD's were outstanding. By 1975, the market had grown tenfold, at an annual compound growth rate in excess of 25 percent. In 1982 the CD market stood at $130 billion (see Figure 3-2).

Thus, large "deposits" began to float through the markets in search of the best rates. But price signals were not the only important matter. Since CD's for amounts in excess of $100,000 were uninsured, negative signals about the stability of any particular bank often caused rapid movements of money, as happened in the case of the Continental Illinois Bank in July 1984; risk-averse and often poorly informed lenders became nervous and disloyal to that bank. It should be pointed out that not all CD money was devoid of relationships. Several banks tried to retain some depositor relationship by marketing CD's directly to major corporate customers. The price at which such transactions took place, however, fully reflected prevailing market conditions.

THE EURODOLLAR MARKET

The development of the CD market gave American bankers a taste for price money. In 1969, when interest-rate ceilings on CD's became binding, American banks moved to the so-called Eurodollar market—a non-U.S. market (in which dollar-denominated deposits and loans were made) that developed during the 1960s—as a means to obtain additional purchased

Figure 3-2
Domestic CD's Outstanding

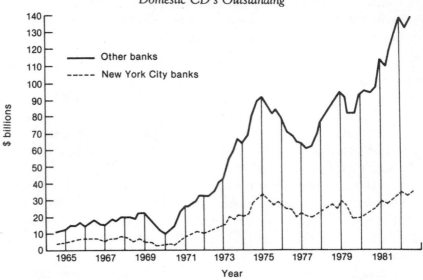

funds.[22] The growth of these essentially unregulated markets has been remarkable. Between 1971 and 1983, the Eurodollar market, which accounts for some 70 to 80 percent of all Eurocurrency transactions, grew at an annual compound growth rate of 25 percent (see Figure 3-3). In the Euromarkets, no central bank has taken a supervisory role for banking behavior, and there is no lender of last resort. National central banks have been aware of this absence of a safety net. In fact, in 1974, a carefully worded statement by the governors of the central banks of the Group of Ten indicated that some unspecified agreement about responsibilities had been reached.[23] Skeptics may well argue, however, that the ambiguity of this statement signalled to the markets that they could continue to operate in an unregulated environment. If a precise and well-defined plan had been presented to allocate responsibilities for the behavior of particular commercial banks to particular central banks, regulation of the Euromarkets would have been inevitable, and the major attraction of the market—its adaptability—would have disappeared.

For commercial banking, the Euromarket alternative—like the alternative to ordinary deposit money provided by the CD market—inevitably led to the decline of the relationship system. The Euromarket and CD market offered large quantities of

Figure 3-3
Euromarkets

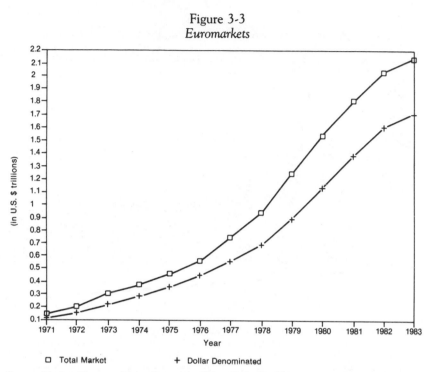

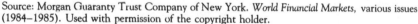

□ Total Market   + Dollar Denominated

Source: Morgan Guaranty Trust Company of New York. *World Financial Markets,* various issues
(1984–1985). Used with permission of the copyright holder.

price-driven money, and at the same time the growth of bankers
acceptances' and of commercial paper markets provided alternatives to traditional credit lines for many customers of the banks.
The stability and relative simplicity of relationships, which had
depended on a lack of financing alternatives, was increasingly
replaced with a complexity in which a variety of price-sensitive
instruments developed. Since the new instruments competed
fiercely on price, and because access to new funds seemed to be
increasingly determined only by price, the value of long-lasting
relationships diminished.

ASSET COMPOSITION OF BANKS

Not surprisingly, as the funding pattern of banks changed, so
did the portfolio of bank assets. (See Table 3-1 and Figure 3-4.)
Looking at the asset composition of the banks over this period, it

Figure 3-4
Selected Assets of Commercial Banks (as a percentage of total assets)

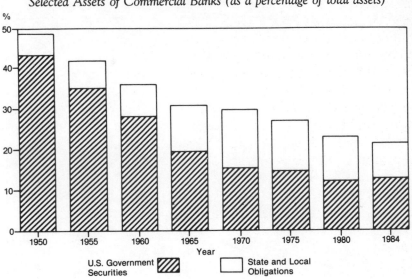

Demand Deposits at Commercial Banks (as a percentage of total liabilities)

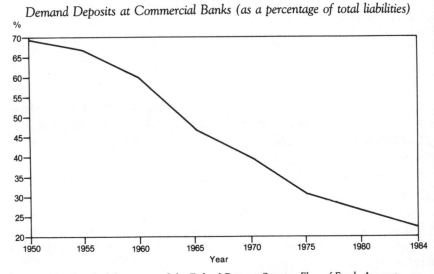

Source: The Board of Governors of the Federal Reserve System, *Flow of Funds Accounts.*

is abundantly clear that bank portfolios gradually began to show more credit risk. While the asset side of the books of the commercial banks showed large holdings of U.S. treasury securities in the first decade after World War II, the ratio between government and private loans fell precipitously thereafter. Over 43 percent of the total assets of banks were invested in government securities in 1950. By 1975, this ratio had dropped to less than 15 percent. Bank loans and consumer credit, on the other hand, represented less than 25 percent in 1954 and more than 40 percent in 1975. In 1984, government securities fell to 13 percent and bank loans and consumer credit rose to 45 percent, thus reversing the positions held in 1950.

This balance sheet restructuring seems natural. During the postwar years, the rapidly expanding U.S. economy created a large commercial loan demand while the need to fund government expenses fell as war-related expenditures came to an end. Thus, the banks reduced their holdings of government securities relative to commercial loans. Furthermore, since banks became increasingly able to "buy" deposit money at will, they could rapidly increase high-yielding commercial loans, which typically also had a higher-risk profile. It is therefore not surprising that, as funding became less relationship- and more price-oriented, the loan portfolio shifted from the government to the private sector and vice versa.

FINANCIAL INNOVATION AND DEREGULATION

Banking reform has always been a complicated topic. In recent years, the process of formal reform of the financial industry has been equally cumbersome.[24] Small wonder then that reform has proved so difficult for both the Senate and the House to enact. Since the financial industry affects every American household and corporation, it is difficult to satisfy (or at least not offend) the major interest groups.

The political difficulty inherent in passing legislation has caused changes in regulation to be reactive rather than proactive. The passage of the Depository Institutions Deregulation and Monetary Control Act (DIDMCA) of 1980 provides a good example: one of its main provisions allowed commercial banks to pay interest on checking accounts (provided some basic requirements were fulfilled by the deposit holder). These so-called NOW and Super NOW accounts allowed banks to respond both to similar accounts that had been offered by thrift institutions and to the increasing competition from the money market mutual funds.

These money market mutual funds are themselves another example of price-oriented instruments. They resemble ordinary deposit accounts, even though they are not quite as liquid. They pay market rates of interest that are offered through fund organizations rather than through banks. The Cash Management Account offered by the securities broker Merrill Lynch was another innovation. It offered money market rates and weekly clearing of a client's brokerage account, it looked at each transaction as an independent price-driven event, but integrating the process. Municipal seven-day demand notes, which began to appear in 1980, are yet another example of price-oriented instruments. They are basically floating-rate notes that give both the borrower and the lender the option to pay off or to recall on five business days' notice. Many other new instruments have been introduced to meet the changing needs of both borrowers and lenders; prices continuously adjust to remain competitive in shifting markets.

The product innovation that took place allowed market participants to avoid relationships and to react to price incentives; it was supplemented by institutional changes that further compromised the segmented nature of the market. Bank holding companies acquired brokerage institutions, even though the Glass-Steagall Act limited these actions. The acquisition of Charles Schwab & Co. by BankAmerica Corporation tested the willingness of the regulators to stretch the interpretation of existing legislation. It is expected that future legislation will provide a more formal framework for regulators to use when they make this kind of decision. Regional conglomeration and even nationwide banking proposals have been advocated by various banks as well as by the chairman of the Federal Reserve.[25] Again, more legislation in this field can be expected, especially since the expanding use of the automated teller machine makes branching restrictions less meaningful and sometimes obsolete.

In the real estate loan sector, the phenomenon of the mortgage-backed security is noteworthy. The sale of securities backed with packages of government-guaranteed mortgages gives investors an opportunity to fully decouple the mortgage relationship that has traditionally been so important between the individual bank and individual customer.[26] The need to fund mortgages with purchased money (money that had to compete with other market-priced instruments) facilitated the development of this market. Thus the "securitization" of a traditional relationship-oriented instrument occurred without a regulatory response. Since then, other loans have begun to be securitized as the move toward more liquid, price-responsive instruments continues.

Overall, financial deregulation has effected many changes in the financial environment.[27] These are now occurring at so great a speed that it is infeasible to make a complete, valuable listing; the U.S. financial system is changing from a slide show to a high-speed film feature! What is clear, however, is that in the new environment traditional relationships have broken down. In their place, price-oriented instruments have attained a forceful presence.

PRICE BANKING AND STABILITY

While we recognize that the United States has moved toward price banking and that regulators have lost some control, the particular effects of this change, especially on the long-term stability of the American financial system, remain difficult to identify. On the one hand, the increased freedom with which financial institutions now operate could create an environment that becomes increasingly stable, as growing diversity in the sources and uses of funds reduces the likelihood of a liquidity crisis. A bank that can buy money in the CD market to infuse liquidity might be able to alleviate the liquidity fears that have led to bank runs in the past. Similarly, if new instruments in the mortgage-lending market allow thrifts to resell their mortgages through mortgage-backed securities, and if the thrifts can write variable-rate mortgages, some of the problems that have traditionally plagued thrifts might be mitigated.[28]

On the other hand, there are also new risks associated with the system, as recent evidence seems to suggest; and there is evidence that the banking system has entered a period of increased instability. Whether such instability will be temporary or will become structurally imbedded in the newly developing system remains to be seen. As banks increase their capacity to fund themselves with purchased, price-sensitive money, the potential for major withdrawals of funds (or for sharp increases in the costs of funding) grows apace. In such an unstable environment, new safeguards may be needed. For example, FDIC deposit insurance is much less effective (if at all) in forestalling liquidity problems because investors in the large CD market are not covered and can withhold their funds.

The role of the FDIC has been a significant one. The institution was founded with two related objectives; the accounts of small depositors were insured so that in the event of major financial disruptions, an element of purchasing power stability was enforced, and at the same time, the insurance itself was expected to lessen the likelihood of instability. As is becoming clear, deposit insurance will continue to tie small depositors to their banks, but in the new environment it is the large depositor who may move away since the relationship tie between him and the institution has been depreciated. During the late 1970s and early 1980s, moreover, the recurrence of bank failures removed the goal of assuring stability as the primary role of deposit insurance; other functions of the FDIC such as assisting troubled banks and overseeing the aftermath of near failures became, increasingly, the FDIC's primary task.

There are numerous examples of the kind of instability that has plagued the financial markets in recent years; here, we mention three. The Penn Central Railroad got into serious problems in 1970, and as is usual in price-oriented markets, the willingness of the market to supply funds to the troubled corporation changed very rapidly. For Penn Central, the commercial paper market quickly dried up, and the company had to activate its backup credit lines with banks. However, the effects of Penn Central's problems spilled over onto other capital users. When the commercial paper market came to fully appreciate that one of the major issuers in this market might actually go bankrupt, it started to question the quality of many of the other issuers as well. As these concerns grew, unrest quickly swept through the commercial paper market and dried up the market for other corporations too.

The speed with which the commercial paper market responded is characteristic of price banking; there are no relationships to slow the reactions of the participants. As companies that normally funded themselves through this market found they could not access it at reasonable prices, they were forced to turn to the banks for backup credit lines. As a result, the demand for bank funds became so large that the Federal Reserve System was forced to provide a major infusion of funds in order to avoid even greater instability in the short-term financing sector.

The second example concerns the 1982 failure of a new, relatively unimportant government securities dealer, Drysdale Government Securities, that had been active in the repurchase (RePo) market.[29] This market, launched in the years after the Second World War, had grown impressively during the late 1970s. It presented yet another example of the shift to price banking. Rather than holding onto assets for a long period of time, the RePo market allowed asset holders to borrow against their assets. Thus, assets could be acquired and immediately financed through RePo's. Drysdale, it now seems clear, engaged in questionable practices to build large positions in RePo's. When the company had to close, amid rumors of large losses, it was significant that Chase Manhattan, an acknowledged expert in government securities, had gotten deeply involved with Drysdale and was forced to take a large write-off against current earnings.[30]

It should be clear from the presentation thus far that it was precisely the reduced importance of stable relationship money and the incessant quest for purchased funds that caused Chase to become deeply involved with Drysdale. The transactions between the two institutions could be seen as purely price-driven events. Unfortunately, the misadventures of Chase's partner, Drysdale, were such that the results generated major losses.

The third example of the new instability occurred in the summer of 1984. This time Continental Illinois Bank of Chicago was the institution that had extensive dealings with a dubious partner (Penn Square Bank). Continental had pursued a rapid growth strategy, relying on purchased money (both CD's and Eurodollars) to fund various originated and purchased loans—a strategy that in itself was hardly novel. In fact, in some quarters the strategy commanded respect: in 1980, *Dun's Review* ranked Continental among the five best-run companies in the United States.

At Penn Square Bank, however, substantial problems emerged, and the associated questionable loans on the books of Continental (in excess of $1 billion) raised suspicions about the viability of the Chicago bank. By the summer of 1984, rumors about the overall quality of Continental's asset portfolio caused a major withdrawal of funds. This time, in contrast to what banks had experienced in the early thirties, the small depositors did not cut and run; they were insured by the FDIC. It was the large CD and foreign depositors that made the exit moves. For these depositors, who had no continuing relationship with the bank and had merely "parked" their money there because of price factors, there was no incentive to stay. They could simply redeposit their holdings in other parts of the money market. When it became clear that Continental was near failure as a consequence of these large depositor withdrawals, the FDIC was forced to insure all depositors, regardless of size; it extracted an equity position in the bank and holding company as partial compensation for its risking potential losses.

Again, the particular incident itself is less important than the two fundamental issues it raises. The first is the issue of the changing composition of bank liabilities. Of Continental's total 1971 assets of $10 billion, CD's and foreign deposits together accounted for only 34 percent; demand deposits, the primary source of relationship money, accounted for another 34 percent. By 1982 purchased money had grown to represent 50 percent of total liabilities and equity. The share of relationship money, as reflected in demand deposits, had fallen to less than 10 percent.

The second issue highlighted by the near failure of the Continental Bank is the limits of protection offered by the FDIC. In a price-banking-oriented world in which large depositors are able to quickly move their assets from institution to institution in search of the most attractive risk-return characteristics, deposit insurance for the small depositor does not provide an effective safeguard for the system. In the new environment the threat to the system comes primarily from the large depositors.

CUSTOMER RELATIONSHIPS UNDER
PRICE BANKING

We have seen that financial products have become increasingly price sensitive and that the value of customer relationships has declined relative to the importance of the ability to offer a product at a competitive price. Theoretically, in a purely price-driven world, the various institutions would offer similar products for similar prices. These prices, reflecting all available information about the product quality, would yield an optimal allocation of the available funds. Nevertheless, there may be a role for a different kind of relationship between the financial intermediary and the borrower or lender.

In a purely price-driven world, such a relationship would give the intermediary *the right to make a bid* for the financial transaction, given a competitive price; this relationship could be developed in many different ways. For example, the ability to offer various financial products from diverse product areas (each of which would have to be priced competitively in accordance with a price-driven world) could allow the intermediary to bid for various aspects of the customer's business. Similarly, in investment banking, a well-established relationship with a client would allow the bank access to the client and thus the opportunity to offer products and services at well-established competitive prices. It is hardly surprising that various commercial banks have created "relationship managers" who try to assure that in the emerging financial world, where customers are predisposed to look for the best prices, the right to sell financial products at prices as attractive as those of the competitors is captured by their particular bank.

It should be stressed that this new type of relationship is fundamentally different from that which characterized the traditional environment prior to the advent of price banking. Traditional relationships were to a large extent substitutes for price competition; the new relationships are complements. In the old system price and product restrictions limited the growth opportunities and assured the profitability of many financial institutions, and thus relationship banking produced slow and careful growth of both assets and liabilities. In the new environment, aggressive pricing policies and innovative behavior can circumvent the traditional boundaries within which the financial institutions historically operated. Relationships are just another tool, similar to aggressive pricing and product development, to attain market share in the price-driven world. As one investment banker recently said, "Often it doesn't matter how long you have known the client. If one of the other firms can offer a deal cheaper, the business is lost."

CONCLUSIONS

This chapter has argued that relationship money, as opposed to price money, was of crucial importance in sustaining the stability and profitability of banks in the past. The relationship system developed over a considerable period of time and was further enhanced by the regulatory reforms of the early 1930s. The outcome of the system was seen in the post–World War II years when American banks were limited in their growth by their inability to form new relationships in a segmented environment that restricted financing alternatives. When interest rates started to rise, and banks wanted to grow more rapidly, it was clear that they could do so only if they could attract money beyond that provided by their traditional customers. Thus, the older forms of financial transactions, which had been based on simple, uninnovative established relationships, gave way to more complex and price-oriented alternatives. This transition occurred both because the costs to the depositor of holding relationship-oriented instruments increased intolerably as nominal rates rose and because the expansion ambitions of the banking intermediaries gathered momentum, especially at times when inflation magnified interest-rate volatility. As those who provided funds tried to obtain the higher returns, disintermediation away from the traditional institutions took place, and alternatives to the traditional relationships appeared. The intermediaries fought back by becoming more innovative. For commercial banks, this meant a move away from a system that was essentially stabilized through relationships and the safety net of small-deposit insurance toward a more volatile system in which banks could (and did) choose the rate at which to grow by purchasing the required funds in the wholesale marketplace.

With the appearance of the CD and Euromarkets, the initial move toward price banking was made, and a further development of other instruments that paid market-determined prices became inevitable because of these competitive pressures. The late 1970s and early 1980s have been characterized by greater innovation, including the securitization of many relationship instruments. Further change seems likely, although its direction is difficult to predict. Two broad possibilities deserve mention. One would return banks to an environment of regulated relationships, not unlike the traditional circumstances from which they have recently emerged. To accomplish this, regulators would have to impose severe restrictions on the businesses open to various groups of institutions. The second alternative, on the other hand, would acknowledge the permanence of price banking and, rather than trying to turn back the clock, would seek acclimatization to the new environment, in part by attempting to create some additional safeguards for the altered system.

New safeguards may well be needed. Already, one implication of the new price-driven environment is that the very largest U.S. banks may enjoy a significant competitive advantage owing to their size. Because failures of large banks do not occur without serious disruption to the overall system, some implicit "systemic guarantee" may well be taken into account by large banks that adopt particularly aggressive loan policies. Thus, as banks increase the asset side of their balance sheets more rapidly in a price-banking environment, this competitive environment carries with it risks that go beyond the stability of individual banks.

For financial institutions themselves, the shift from relationship banking to price banking has transformed the financial environment from a simple, static, and price-regulated world to one that is complex, innovative, and increasingly price competitive. In this unfamiliar environment new skills are required to exploit new opportunities. And while the new order carries the risk of possible failure, the possible rewards of rapid growth and enhanced profitability are also present.

Although regulators have observed signs of increased instability introduced into the financial system by the new competitive forces, they have not effectively reversed the trend; the incentives to escape from regulatory control have become too great; the interaction with unregulated foreign markets is too pervasive; and the general appeal of deregulation in many industries is too strong. Further, regulators may have been favorably impressed by the effects of a price-driven system that helps eliminate distortions in the market allocation of capital and thereby presumably provides consumers with cheaper, more varied, and more efficient financial products and services. For the regulators, perhaps the main source of disquiet lies in their loss of control over events, and the implications that flow from possible market responses to the misadventures of financial entrepreneurs; the speed with which instability can spread throughout the system is indeed sobering.

The evolution of the American financial system not only poses challenges to financial intermediaries and their customers, it also challenges regulators. There will undoubtedly be some regulatory changes. For example, the role of the FDIC clearly must change; under price banking, providing deposit insurance for small deposits is like offering *fire* insurance for a house threatened by *floods*. The policy of the FDIC with respect to potential failures at large banks needs to be reexamined and redefined.

A new, asset-based deposit insurance scheme might be set up whereby the deposit insurance premium would relate to the quality of the bank's assets. Such a policy could deal with the effects of the "systemic guarantee" mentioned earlier. A major problem with such a policy, however, is the classification of the assets of the banks in risk categories that are acceptable to both the regulators and the affected banks. Private rating agencies could develop criteria in a manner similar to that employed for the recently introduced ratings of certificates of deposits. Another avenue might stress new minimum capital requirements (set by regulators) that relate (for instance) to both the growth rate and quality of bank assets.

It will not, of course, be easy to implement new procedures for enhancing the stability of the financial system in a price-driven world, particularly as financial institutions increasingly diversify to broaden their funding base. The notion of the "financial supermarket" has sprung up as a result of existing institutions merging across traditional product lines. These institutions would offer many financial services and, in theory, would have access to a funding base diversified by both geographic and product categories. Some observers believe that such diversification would generate greater public confidence by virtue of the size and ability of these broad institutions to attract funds from diverse areas. The example of several European nations where large "universal" banks dominate the financial markets provides a model.

Many questions remain. Aside from questions of capital funding for a series of acquisitions, it should be noted that the notion of a financial supermarket or a geographically diversified bank has not yet proved to be a viable concept in the United States. The success of recent conglomerations is at best debatable; some of these institutions have found it difficult to retain many of the most attractive characteristics of the acquired entities. The change in orientation at Dean Witter after its takeover by Sears provides one case in point. Similarly, the acquisition of Lehman Brothers by American Express caused a major change in the corporate culture of Lehman, despite elaborate legal agreements that were aimed at ensuring that the company retain both its character and its human resources assets. The recently announced divestiture of parts of its real estate business by Merrill Lynch shows that at least one of the front-runners in the development of the broadly diversified financial institution has itself had second thoughts. Perhaps most important, it is not clear that such larger institutions would be tolerated in the United States, which (as I have noted) is traditionally suspicious of central and concentrated financial control. In other words, it is not clear how much deregulation and conglomeration Congress will allow.

The shift from relationship to price banking has opened a new chapter in the evolution of the U.S. financial system. It seems clear that the development of the financial system will continue to be characterized by product innovation and reliance on price-competitive markets that are inherently less stable than traditional relationship banking. The challenge for regulators, financial intermediaries, and the public is to reestablish stability while still allowing market forces to continue to play their constructive role.

NOTES

1. The following references provide accounts of the development of the U.S. financial system; Albert Bolles, *The Financial History of the United States, 1774–1885.* 3 vols. (New York: Appleton, 1883–1886); Herman E. Krooss, *Documentary History of Banking and Currency in the United States.* 4 vols. (New York: Chelsea House, 1969); Fritz Redlich, *The Molding of American Banking: Men and Ideas.* 2 vols. (New York: Hafner, 1940); Herman E. Krooss, et al., *A History of Financial Intermediaries* (New York: Random House, 1971); Margaret G. Myers, *A Financial History of the United States* (New York: Columbia University Press, 1970); William J. Shultz, et al., *Financial Development of the United States* (New York: Prentice-Hall, 1937); Benjamin Klebaner, *Commercial Banking in the United States: A History* (Hinsdale, Ill.: Dryden Press, 1974); Paul Studenski, et al., *Financial History of the United States* (New York: McGraw-Hill, 1963); Bray Hammond, *Banks and Politics in America from the Revolution to the Civil War* (Princeton, N.J.: Princeton University Press, 1957).

2. On the view that state banks safeguard the banking system from highly centralized federal government control, see, for example, Thomas W. Thompson, *Checks and Balances: A Study of the Dual Banking System in America.* National Association of Supervisors of State Banks. (Washington, D.C., 1962), chap. 6 (especially p. 71).

3. Various states were so opposed to the national bank that they levied discriminatory taxes against it. See Shultz, *Financial Development of the United States,* chap. 8.

4. For remarks on this "most profound descent into indiscretion," see Bray Hammond, *Banks and Politics in America,* p. 297.

5. On duality in the U.S. banking system, see William J. Brown, *The Dual Banking System in the United States* (New York: American Bankers Association, 1969), and Thomas W. Thompson, *Checks and Balances.* There were incentives for banks to retain a state charter, even though it meant foregoing the privileges associated with membership; for example, the reserve requirements for national banks were typically higher than those set on the state level, and certain product areas were not open to national banks. For a discussion of the National Banking Act and its effects, see Andrew M. Davis, *The Origin of the National Banking System.* National Monetary Commission Report. (Washington, D.C., 1910), and William W. Swanson, *The Establishment of the National Banking System* (Kingston: Jackson Press, 1910).

6. The introduction in 1865 of a tax law that levied a 10 percent surcharge on the state issues drove them out of existence. See Shultz, *Financial Development of the United States,* pp. 316–18, 348.

7. Quoted in Alfred D. Chandler, Jr., et al., *The Coming of Managerial Capitalism, A Casebook on the History of American Economic Institutions* (Homewood, Ill.: Richard D. Irwin, Inc., 1985), case 10, p. 286.

8. The Aldrich-Freeland Act of 1908 allowed for special note issuance in times of financial distress. It also created a National Monetary Commission to study banking abroad. See Shultz, *Financial Development of the United States,* p. 473.

9. For accounts of the creation and development of the Federal Reserve System, see Roger T. Johnson, *Historical Beginnings: The Federal Reserve* (Boston: Federal Reserve Bank of Boston, 1979); Federal Reserve Bank of Philadelphia. *Fifty Years of the Federal Reserve Act* (Philadelphia, 1964); Milton Friedman, et al., *A Monetary History of the United States, 1867–1960* (Princeton, N.J.: Princeton University Press, 1963); The Board of Governors of the Federal Reserve System. *The Federal Reserve System: Purposes and Functions* (Washington, D.C.: Federal Reserve Board, 1974).

10. On challenges to the banking system brought about by the Depression, and subsequent reform measures, see Friedman et al., *A Monetary History of the United States, 1867–1960,* chaps. 7–8; Shultz, *Financial Development of the United States,* chaps. 27–29; Friedman et al., *The Great Contractions, 1929–1933* (Princeton, N.J.: Princeton University Press,

1965); Peter Temin, *Did Monetary Forces Cause the Great Depression?* (New York: W. W. Norton, 1976).

11. For the effects of Regulation Q, see Charles F. Haywood, et al., *The Regulation of Deposit Interest Rates.* Association of Reserve City Bankers. (Chicago, 1968); and Charles F. Haywood, *Regulation Q and Monetary Policy.* Association of Reserve City Bankers. (Chicago, 1971).

12. See Friedman, et al., *A Monetary History of the United States,* pp. 438–39.

13. See the FDIC Annual Report (Washington, D.C., 1984).

14. For a similar interpretation, see U.S. Treasury Department, Report of the President, *Geographic Restrictions on Commercial Banking in the U.S.* (Washington, D.C., 1981), pp. 1, 2.

15. For a brief description of these regulations, see Tim S. Campbell, *Financial Institutions, Markets and Economic Activity* (New York: McGraw-Hill, 1982), pp. 444–59.

16. See Marcia Stigum, *The Money Market.* 3rd ed. (Homewood, Ill.: Dow-Jones Irwin, 1983), chap. 5.

17. See Jay O. Light, et al., *The Financial System* (Homewood, Ill.: Richard D. Irwin, 1979), pp. 336–39. In more recent years the equity market has actually become a user of corporate funds rather than a source of funds. As many corporations considered their stocks undervalued they repurchased stock. Similarly, stocks were purchased by institutions fearing hostile takeovers.

18. See M. Colyer Crum, et al., "From Relationship to Price Banking: The Loss of Regulatory Control" in *America vs. Japan,* T. K. McCraw, ed. (Boston: Harvard Business School Press, 1986).

19. The role of the Federal Reserve had been to peg the interest rate; in the wake of the outbreak of the Korean war, fear of inflation increased, and the Federal Reserve decided that the low interest rate policy favored by the Treasury was no longer possible. After a public controversy with the Treasury, the Federal Reserve regained the power to follow an independent interest rate policy. An accord was issued to this effect on March 4, 1951. See Lester V. Chandler, *The Economics of Money and Banking.* 6th ed. (New York: Harper & Row, 1973), chap. 24.

20. For a description of the CD market, see Stigum, *The Money Market,* chap. 15.

21. Harold van B. Cleveland and Thomas F. Huertas, *Citibank 1812–1970* (Cambridge, Mass.: Harvard University Press, 1985), p. 256.

22. On the development of the Eurocurrency markets, see Stigum, *The Money Market,* chaps. 6, 15, 16; and Daniel R. Kane, *The Eurodollar Market and the Years of Crisis* (London: Croom Helm, 1983). The name "Eurodollar" (and other currency designations with the prefix "Euro-") refers to a deposit or loan made in a currency other than the one of the country in which the bank that takes the deposit or makes the loan is located. See G. L. Bell, *The Eurodollar Market and the International Financial System* (New York: Macmillan, 1973); and Stigum, *The Money Market,* pp. 175–80.

23. Stigum, *The Money Market,* pp. 179–80.

24. See Sidney L. Jones, *The Development of Economic Policy: Financial Institution Reform* (Ann Arbor: University of Michigan Press, 1979), especially chaps. 5, 8, 9.

25. *New York Times,* April 25, 1985, p. D1.

26. For a brief description of the various mortgage instruments and their markets, see Roland I. Robinson, et al., *Financial Markets: The Accumulation and Allocation of Wealth* (New York: McGraw-Hill, 1980), chap. 15.

27. On U.S. financial deregulation in the early 1980s, see Alan Gart, *The Insider's Guide to the Financial Services Revolution* (New York: McGraw-Hill, 1984); George J. Benston, ed., *Financial Services: The Changing Institutions and Government Policy* (Englewood Cliffs, N.J.: Prentice-Hall, 1983); *Harvard Business Review,* ed., *The Transformation of Banking* (Boston, Mass.: Harvard Business School, 1984); Stigum, *The Money Market;* Andrew S. Carron,

Reforming the Bank Regulatory Structure (Washington, D.C.: Brookings Institution, 1984); and *Economic Report of the President* (Washington, D.C.: GPO, 1984), chap. 5.

28. The problems that have plagued the thrifts are not surprising. With long-term assets and short-term liabilities, the thrifts were easily profitable when the yield curve had its usual shape and interest rates were stable; it was during the 1970s, when the yield curve started to show unusual behavior and interest rates rose rapidly, that their long-term commitments became very expensive. As a result, the thrifts found it difficult to be profitable. See Andrew S. Carron, *The Plight of the Thrift Institution* (Washington, D.C.: Brookings Institution, 1982).

29. For an account of the events at Drysdale, see *Institutional Investor* (September 1982).

30. Chase Manhattan at first refused to carry the losses associated with the Drysdale debacle because of the ambiguous legal status of the RePo, but it later reversed itself.

FOUR

THE INSTITUTIONALIZATION OF WEALTH: CHANGING PATTERNS OF INVESTMENT DECISION MAKING

Jay O. Light and Andre F. Perold

Throughout the last three decades, the pool of institutionally owned funds has grown substantially. Pension funds, particularly corporate pension funds, have been the most important element of this growth; but other institutional owners have also grown and have shifted their assets toward common stocks. As a result, the equity holdings of pension funds and other institutional owners have become a significant percentage of all equities outstanding (see Table 4-1).

As more of the wealth of the country has flowed toward these very large pension pools, investment decision making has become much more concentrated. Indeed, by the mid-1970s it had already become commonplace to speak of the growing "institutional dominance" of the equity markets. Many ills (both real and imagined) of our current marketplace have been blamed on this trend toward institutional ownership and calls for a regulatory response have been recurrent.

In this chapter, we will analyze and illustrate a number of the salient changes that have occurred in the patterns of investment decision making, trading activity, and financial markets as a result of this trend toward institutional ownership. In particular, we will describe the changes in who makes the decisions, in the structure and strategy of investment organizations, in the level and focus of active investment decisions, in the growing complexity of program trading and other transaction strategies of institutional investors, in the separate growth of index futures and other derivative securities available for investment transactions, and in the ways in which all of these work together to segment and alter financial markets, including particularly the equity market.

The final section of the chapter will address some of the questions, problems, and opportunities that these developments present for a number of different market participants and public

Table 4-1
Institutional Ownership of Assets

	1955	1960	1965	1970	1975	1980	1985
Total Pension Fund Holdings (in $ billions)							
All assets	27	58	108	171	252	485	1,102
Equities	5	17	43	77	113	220	499
Equity Holdings As a Percent of All Equities Outstanding							
Pension Funds	2	4	6	9	13	14	22
Households	91	87	84	79	74	73	60

Source: Federal Reserve *Flow of Funds Accounts.*

policy formulators. It is particularly important to sort out the regulatory implications of this fundamental change in market structure. There will undoubtedly be some fine-tuning required in the rule making and statutory fabric of industry oversight. But the deliberations surrounding these regulatory changes should recognize that the shifts in institutional investors' decision making chronicled in this chapter are fundamental, far-reaching, and not likely to be transitory.

THE OLD SYSTEM OF PENSION MANAGEMENT

Though the inflows into corporate pension funds had been proceeding in earnest since the 1950s, the system by which these pension funds were managed was surprisingly slow to change. In the first stages of their development, corporate pension funds employed investment management firms in the same way that earlier client groups (for example, wealthy families) had done for decades. Typically, they retained one (and sometimes several) large, well-established institutions to cautiously manage balanced portfolios (portfolios with both stocks and bonds, and perhaps cash) with relatively little turnover. The money managers generally performed all of the facets of a complete bundled investment service, just as they did for their traditional individual and family clients. They set the asset mix, picked the stocks, diversified appropriately across both industries and sectors, and did the trading; they also provided discussions of the market outlook, and might occasionally have attempted a little market timing. They nurtured relationships and tried to build multiple ties to their new corporate pension clients. They often dealt with the client across a range of other services (banking, for example, in the case of bank trust departments). They were investment counselors and advisers in the traditional sense of those terms and were relatively undifferentiated among each other in their services and in their basic approach to investing.

In the world of trading, of course, commissions were fixed. Indeed, they were fixed at a level substantially higher than actual costs warranted. In return, brokerage firms provided a host of services under this fixed-pricing umbrella, including most importantly execution. Specifically, institutional money management firms could trade substantial blocks of individual stocks with little or no price impact and thus create the illusion of relatively easy and frictionless trading for the active trader, even for large-sized transactions.

In this environment, trading within the money management firm was often treated as a relatively technical, semiclerical activity. In effect, trading was accomplished in a fixed-price, one-stock-at-a-time environment where the potentially interesting interplay between traders with different motives and different philosophies was hidden in the cushion of fixed commissions.

THE DEVELOPMENT OF IN-HOUSE DECISION MAKING

As the growth of institutional money in general and pension funds in particular continued, though, the money management business itself began to evolve in important ways from the earlier, undifferentiated, relationship-intensive business described above. First, as these pools grew larger, their long-run impact upon the overall financial health of the sponsoring corporation (or other enterprise) became obviously more important.

Second, corporate clients began to doubt the ability of their large traditional money management firms to outperform the market. These doubts were heightened by the collapse of the two-tier market in the early 1970s and the overall collapse of the equity market in 1973–1974; in both periods many well-regarded institutional money managers failed to protect their clients. As a result, clients began to wonder whether their reliance on external money management professionals was the most effective way to manage large pools of capital. Moreover, these clients were becoming more concerned with the often subtle but nonetheless real divergences between their own best interest and the business interests of their money managers. Finally, the passage of ERISA in 1974 forced corporations to take a more proactive role in the management of their pension funds by, in effect, requiring that they formulate, articulate, and document their investment policy for the fund as a whole.

The influence of these forces resulted in two of the most important changes in the money management business: the growth of in-house pension staffs and the birth of the pension-consulting business.[1] Figures 4-1a and 4-1b illustrate the recent evolution of corporate pension staffs in large corporations. Figure 4-1a represents the earlier relationship between the external money managers and the corporation in which the board of directors and a senior financial officer usually managed the fund. Given their other responsibilities, the total time these people could actually spend on pension matters was severely limited. And that, of course, was a large part of the problem. Thus, as the first step of the evolution toward the new decision-making structure represented in Figure 4-1b, the corporation typically established a pension committee(s) that reported to the board (and perhaps included one or two board members), and assumed regular pension oversight. Second, a full-time pension officer was appointed to manage the pension function on a day-to-day basis and to report to the pension committee and the chief financial officer. Next, the pension officer hired several people to serve as his/her internal staff. And finally, this newly structured, in-house group hired one or more external consulting firms to help them on a continuing basis with the job of managing the pension function.

These pension staffs were built, of course, to formulate a policy for managing the pension assets in very broad terms and to hire and monitor the external money management firms. Once these organizational units were in place, however, it was inevitable that most of the important asset-management deci-

Figure 4-1
The Evolving Internal Pension Structure

a. The Prototypical Earlier Relationship

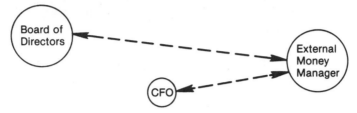

b. The Prototypical Current Structure

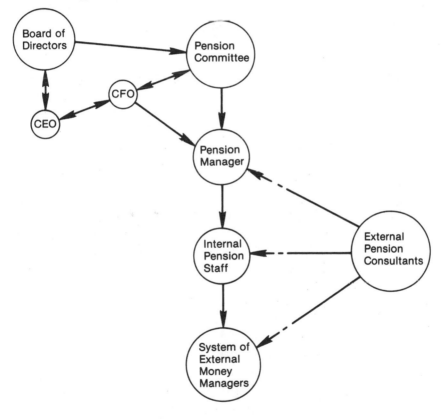

sions would be moved in-house away from the external money managers. Today this transformation has generally been completed in many if not most sizable corporate pension plans. For these plans, the role of the appropriate long-run asset allocation is now decided almost exclusively in-house, sometimes with the help of pension consultants who often provide technical support in the form of asset-liability simulations. The investment policy within respective asset types (e.g., selecting the average maturity of the fixed-income segment, or the average yield or growth orientation of the equity segment, or the percentage of foreign equities) is generally specified by the in-house organization and implemented through the choice of particular money managers. Indeed, through the choice of money managers whose portfolio specialties conform to particular guidelines, the in-house organizations now make most of the important decisions that might in earlier years have fallen under the general label of investment counseling. In most cases, what is left for the external money managers is the individual stock picking and perhaps a little market timing, and usually even these decisions are made in the relatively circumscribed ways that the corporation and the external manager have already agreed upon.

In many ways, this evolution is entirely appropriate, of course, for only the pension plan sponsor is (and should be) held responsible for the most basic investment policy decisions. Moving these broad or "macro" decisions in-house ensures the ability to tailor a specific investment policy to the financial needs of the pension plan and the plan sponsor. Indeed, these changes have ushered in an era of much more active macro management by corporate pension staffs. For example, through bond immunization and dedication approaches,[2] fixed-income portfolios have been tailored to the particular demographics of a pension plan's retired population. In addition, asset shifts toward these and other fixed-income portfolios have been used to help rationalize substantial reductions of funding for corporations in severe financial distress. Sometimes such funding reductions (and, in extreme cases, plan terminations and asset reversions) have been used to thwart the threat of unwanted takeovers. In contrast, other corporations have attempted to maximize funding and manage the fund so as to minimize taxes and/or maximize the financial slack that the corporation can store off the balance sheet in a tax-deferred form. In general, corporations have come to see the investment policy of the pension fund as an integral part of the overall corporate financial policy and have begun to manage it as such.

The recent changes in financial reporting standards for pension funds (FASB 87 and 88, released in January 1986) will clearly accelerate this trend. They will require fuller and more uniform disclosure of pension assets, liabilities, and expenses, and thus make companies even more concerned with the financial impact of their pension decisions. In addition, for some companies there will be a new and quite visible liability on the balance sheet itself; these companies will clearly strive to manage their pension assets relative to their liabilities so as to control the balance sheet impact of their pension plan.

As part of the implementation of investment policy, a basic function of the corporate pension staff is to hire, monitor, and evaluate the external managers and when sufficiently dissatisfied, to replace them. As they search for superior performance, the in-house pension managers have thus begun to manage large "portfolios" of money management firms in much the same way as portfolio managers in search of the same objective manage portfolios of stocks. In fact, some of the larger corporate plan sponsors now employ more than fifty external managers. There is also a clear trend toward the selection of active money management firms with a specialized and highly differentiated (perhaps unique) approach to selecting securities. Although the dimensions along which this differentiation (aggravatingly referred to as "style") occurs are complex, they include at least:

1. The *type* of companies a firm invests in
   (e.g., small companies, or large-growth companies, or regional bank stocks).
2. The *level* of selection decisions
   (e.g., stock picking, or industry selection, or sector timing).
3. The competitive edge employed in the selection process
   (e.g., superior but perishable information, better valuation frameworks, etc.).

Let us take a closer look at the prototypical multiple-manager system illustrated in Figure 4-2. In this example, the in-house

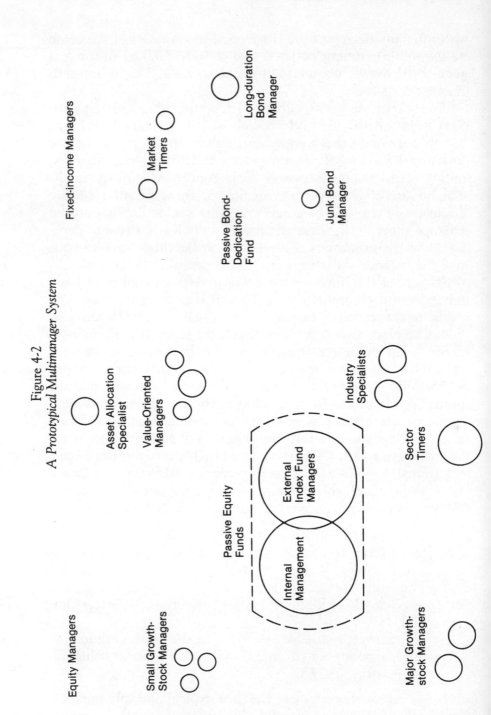

Figure 4-2
A Prototypical Multimanager System

pension staff has first established the asset allocation between equities and bonds, as well as the normal investment targets for each. Within this framework, the staff might then choose an "active-passive" allocation. Usually with the help of consultants, the staff will select a variety of specialty managers to receive the active funds. The passive funds might be distributed to one or more external firms that provide indexed products— either straightforward, low-cost index funds or mildly managed variants (for example, index funds that are tilted toward higher yield or those that trade back and forth between futures and stocks, depending upon pricing, etc.). Rarely, if ever, is 100 percent of the fund turned over to passive managers (as might be advocated by devotees of efficient market theories). Instead, the role of the passive fund(s) is to unbundle the diversification function from the stock-picking function and to provide simple, low-cost diversification that complements the system's multiple, active managers.

In addition, these passive funds are beginning to be used to align the overall exposure of the composite portfolio with various dimensions of investment policy. Consider, for example, a plan sponsor organized around a multiple-manager approach as depicted in Figure 4-2. Suppose this sponsor wants to hire a group of specialty, active equity managers whose portfolios characteristically (and collectively) have a pronounced small-stock bias. If the sponsor wants to bet on small stocks, then this might be an appropriate structuring of his equity portfolio. If on the other hand, he only wants to hire the managers for their stock-picking ability within small stocks and wishes to keep his stocks neutral with respect to company size, then, additionally, he will need to hold some large-company stocks. This can easily be accomplished with the passive fund by turning it into a so-called "completeness fund" (a more carefully tailored index fund that overweights large stocks). In addition, in constructing this passive portfolio, the sponsor may want to compensate not only for small-company risk, but also for other risks that are being unintentionally taken by the collection of specialty managers. In general, the sponsor can construct a total passive portfolio that balances the risk factors of the portfolios of the individual managers, and thus provides centralized macro control of the portfolio's overall investment policy.

THE TRANSFORMATION OF THE MONEY
MANAGEMENT BUSINESS

These changing pension client needs have dramatically changed the strategies of some money management firms and the structure of the money management business. The older established firms and, more important, the new entrants have sharpened their image as specialists and have attempted to differentiate themselves further from their competitors.

The active and passive management sectors are clearly in the process of almost completely separating, and very few firms have been successful in both sectors. Each sector is developing in much the way that might have been predicted on the basis of the factors outlined above.

The rapidly growing passive business has been developing in both stocks (with the plain-vanilla S&P 500 index funds and a variety of more complex, but still passive, schemes—some of which were described above), and in fixed-income securities based on immunization, dedication, and other specially tailored but passive strategies.[3] With the availability of new, computer-based technology, even relatively esoteric passive strategies can be implemented routinely and extremely cheaply with large pools of capital. The passive business is a low-cost, low-fee, high-tech, commoditylike business with considerable economies of scale. Not surprisingly, therefore, it has come to be dominated by a small number of low-cost firms, each with very substantial pools of capital under management.

As the number of firms and their different approaches to investments proliferate, the active business has been developing in exactly the opposite direction. And it is easy to see why. Large firms with many professionals and a large, established client base are continually tempted to try to be too many things to too many people. Small firms can more effectively formulate and credibly implement the kind of simple, distinctive investment approach that appeals to more and more corporate pension clients. In addition, active management requires active trading, and there can be significant diseconomies of scale in the trading phase of money management because larger transactions can cause more substantial price impacts. Finally, new communications and computing technology allows even very small firms to perform many of the same tasks that only large firms could afford to tackle in earlier years. In a number of the market's niches, particularly in those whose highly differentiated approaches lend themselves easily to the use of this new technology, the number of firms has increased dramatically. By the end of 1985 the number of separate money management firms managing more than $100 million in tax-exempt (mostly pension) assets had grown to more than 500.[4]

While the barriers to entry in the active pension management business have thus been very small, there are more significant barriers to continued growth and long-lived success.[5] In the active management business, the performance records of money managers are increasingly compared on a quarter-to-quarter and year-to-year basis, despite the obvious problems of using such short-term time horizons. The records of money managers with similar styles are compared in a kind of performance derby, as pension plan sponsors and their consultants decide whom to hire and (occasionally) whom to fire. A good "story" about recent relative performance is an essential, as is a simple but distinctive approach to money management. And this places substantial near-term performance pressures on the active money managers, particularly the host of relatively new entrants to the business.

Consultants have come to play a large role in the manager selection process; in fact, this role has grown to the point where the consultant has become a de facto money-manager "broker." Consulting firms compete with each other to characterize money management firms on new and revealing dimensions and to promote their current favorites among each closely related group; their blessing is often the source of a start-up money management firm's first institutional account. Relegation by the consultants to also-ran status is often the last straw triggering substantial account withdrawals. Not surprisingly, this power has led to consultants being intensively courted by money managers, and particularly by the specialty managers.[6]

These changes have also created a new and very different character to the trading needs of pension funds, and their turnover rates have increased dramatically. The macro decisions of the in-house pension staffs have contributed to this turnover, as funds are shifted from fixed income to equities, or from equities back to a dedicated bond portfolio. In addition, the rate at which active managers are hired and replaced in the performance derby has further contributed to this turnover. Finally, the turnover rates of individual money managers have increased substantially in response to the need to consistently demonstrate superior performance. The aggregate turnover rate for the New York Stock Exchange (NYSE) reflects these changes (see Table 4-2):

Table 4-2
New York Stock Exchange Trading

Year	Average Daily Share Volume (millions of shares)	Turnover Rate (%)	Large Trades of 10,000 Shares (% of total volume)
1960	3.0	12	NA
1965	6.2	14	3
1970	11.6	19	15
1975	18.6	21	17
1980	44.9	36	29
1985	109.2	54	52

Source: NYSE, Fact Book 1986, pp. 69, 70, 71.

One can observe that trading and turnover have increased sharply, particularly during the last decade. In 1986, trading volume and turnover rates were substantially higher than in 1985. In addition, as the last column in Table 4-2 demonstrates, the relative importance of large trades has also grown dramatically; of course, much of institutional trading is still done in trades of less than 10,000 shares, so that the last column considerably understates the relative importance of institutional trading. It is believed that probably more than 80 percent of the expanded trading volume on the NYSE is now attributable to institutions (a sharp increase from the percentage of just 10 years ago).

THE ALTERED COMMISSION STRUCTURE

While this transformation was under way, the structure of commissions, the most visible cost of trading, has changed substantially. It is well known that some segments of the institutional community were not at all happy with the fixed commission structure that existed prior to 1975. By channeling some of their trading through third market (non-NYSE) firms and clamoring for their own memberships on the exchange, they created pressures for change. These pressures, coupled with Justice Department concern, led to the abolishment of fixed commissions in May 1975.

Since then the average commissions paid by institutional traders have headed downward, pausing intermittently at various levels. From something like 25 to 30¢ (for the typical $30 stock) in the pre–1975 era, commissions probably averaged less than 9¢ in 1985, or about 30 percent of their former levels. Moreover, there is a range of commissions around the average paid by individual money management firms, and the amount of a particular commission depends on the strategy and the difficulty of particular trades. "Easy" trades (that is, trades that can be done with little or no price impact) can be channeled through brokerage firms for about a 9¢ payment for research and other services. Easy trades are also done for substantially lower commissions when no ancillary services are involved. As might be expected in a negotiated rate environment, money management firms have begun to face difficult decisions involving the commission structure that they are willing to support and the bundles of services, if any, that they will "buy" with these commissions.

More important for our present discussion, the erosion of commissions has made the price impact of "difficult" transactions more visible. To be sure, execution had always been an important element of trading, and price had been the key to judging execution. In the over-the-counter (OTC) market (a dealer market), price was the only determinant of net trading cost; the bid-ask spread of the dealer played the role of a commission. But when dealing in NYSE stocks, much of the price impact had been hidden within the relatively high commissions on the NYSE. As commissions dropped, brokers experienced greatly increased difficulty covering expected trading losses with these commissions. Furthermore, money management firms had the habit of sending easy trades to particular brokers in payment for various services, and this left a dwindling number of brokers to handle the more difficult trades. And demand for execution of the more difficult trades was increasing in direct proportion to the growth in turnover rates and the growth in average trade size. With the erosion of the commission structure, price became an active element in the negotiations to execute these trades. Given this evolution, the execution skills of a money manager's trading desk became an important element of overall investment performance.

This evolution in commission structure had an important influence on the pension fund clients of money management firms as well as on the boards of directors of mutual funds. By the 1980s money managers no longer presented an undifferentiated perspective on transaction costs. Some money management firms paid very low commissions, while others paid substantially higher commissions. Most money management firms claimed very low execution costs (including price impact), and some of these firms provided extensive studies in an effort to prove their claims. As part of their continuing oversight responsibilities, clients have now become very interested in both the level of commissions and the execution costs that money management firms incur. Indeed, the transaction-cost measurement business, in which consultants attempt to measure and evaluate the overall transactions costs (commissions plus price impact) of various money management firms, has become one of the most rapidly growing (even though it is still small) sectors within the market for investment services.

THE CHANGING WORLD OF INSTITUTIONAL TRANSACTIONS

The patterns of institutional transactions have changed as turnover rates have increased, the investment approaches of money managers have become more differentiated, and the price impacts of their transactions have become more visible and more important. Pension staffs, money managers, and brokers have tried to improve the match between the tactics and techniques of trading and particular investment decisions and to minimize the more visible aspects of price impact. Transactions used to take place almost exclusively on a stock-by-stock basis, but this is no longer true. By some estimates, something like a quarter or more of all institutional trading today is accomplished in various types of "program trades" (simultaneous or nearly simultaneous trades of large packages of many different securities). In particular, almost all of the trading triggered by the macro decisions of pension plan sponsors takes place in the form of these program trades.

For example, when the in-house pension managers decide to shift funds from common stocks to a dedicated bond portfolio (perhaps as part of a major corporate financial policy change), literally hundreds of stocks (perhaps the whole S&P 500 stock universe) may have to be sold and hundreds of bonds may have to be bought. These restructuring trades are typically accomplished by packaging them into one major program trade, or restructuring, for which both a commission and a set of prices relative to some future (and therefore unknown) set of closing prices are put out for bids from competing brokers. Or, for example, when the in-house pension staff decides to change equity managers, major sales and purchases of stocks again take place. These stocks, too, are typically packaged into a major program trade; the in-house staff or the new money manager structures the terms of a swap that will either be put out for bids from a number of brokers or else negotiated with a single broker. The ways in which these trades are structured, and the tactics of the bidding or negotiation process, are constantly being altered in the ongoing evolution of the "art" of program trading.

In addition, individual investment management firms are now beginning to use program trades for their own purposes. For example, when a firm wants to rotate its holdings from one classically defined sector to another (e.g., sell the chemicals and buy the autos), or switch from one investment strategy to another (e.g., sell small-growth companies and buy large multinational companies with significant exposure to changing exchange rates), packaging the entire transaction into one large program trade may be the preferred execution alternative. Indeed, money management firms are increasingly performing such investment shifts as an important dimension of their distinctive investment approach. And an increasing number of these shifts are taking the form of prenegotiated program trades.

Not only is the level of trading changing from that which is characteristic of the traditional stock-by-stock trades, but as firms' decision-making processes have become more differentiated, so have their trading needs along a number of other dimen-

Figure 4-3
Typology of Institutional Trading Needs

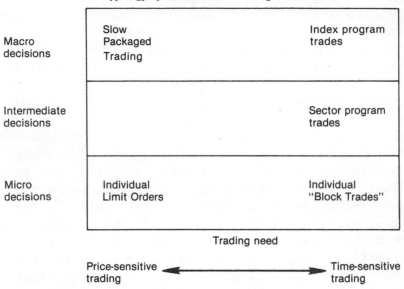

sions. Figure 4-3 illustrates one possible typology of these trading needs.

Consider first the lower right-hand corner of this conceptual map: imagine a portfolio manager who wants to sell stock in XYZ Corp. because he has gotten wind of developments likely to lower its next quarter's earnings. Clearly he will want to get out quickly and may be willing to compromise a little on price. The typical vehicle for such a transaction need is the "block trade," in which the broker either finds the other side of the trade (an agency trade) or buys some or all of the stock himself (a principal trade) with the expectation of finding a buyer in the near future.

Consider next the lower left-hand corner of Figure 4-3, the natural habitat of the value-oriented stock picker: imagine a portfolio manager who invests in companies when they appear cheap on the basis of some criteria such as P/E's, or price-to-book value ratios, or price-to-liquidation value ratios, or perhaps relative to the value estimated by a model that discounts the projected stream of future cash dividends. Imagine further that as the price of XYZ is driven down (perhaps by the earnings-forecasting investor described above), it begins to look very attractive in light of the value-oriented investor's particular valuation methodology. He wants to buy XYZ, but is likely to use a quite different strategy than our first investor. He should be quite indifferent to the time of the trade: today is okay, but so is tomorrow, or next month. The important variable for him is price. In particular, he wants to trade only at a price that compensates him adequately for the possibility that the forecasters driving the price down really do know something.[7] To trade effectively, he should think in terms of this price and articulate his trading in the form of "limit orders" to buy only at this price. Note that in some sense these value-oriented traders are the real "market makers" in our capital markets—those traders who are ultimately willing to hold financial assets in the presence of disturbing developments or forecasts and who are also willing to sell assets in the presence of encouraging developments or forecasts.[8]

These same distinctions between time-sensitive and price-sensitive trading techniques extend to the more aggregated types of package trading represented at the top of Figure 4-3. Consider, for example, an index fund manager who will begin managing a $500-million account indexed to the S&P 500 Index as of July 1. Competitive performance within the indexing business is measured along two dimensions: costs (including commissions) and tracking accuracy (how closely the performance of the index fund matches that of the index). The indexer wants to make sure that the pension client sees that the fund tracks the S&P 500 Index precisely beginning on July 1. This will require "getting in" at prices exactly equal to those at the market's close on June 30. The solution is simple: execute a program trade in which the broker guarantees that the trade will occur at those (still) unknown future prices in exchange for a negotiated commission. This is, of course, a very time-sensitive, but not a price-sensitive, trade. The fund manager wants to buy at precisely 4:00 p.m. on June 30, at the closing prices, but cares very little about those prices in any absolute sense. By compressing his buying toward the end of the trading session on June 30, the broker merely raises the level of the market to let the new $500 million in or (in a program sale) lowers the level of the market to let the $500 million out. While at first glance these program trades appear to be very different from the block trades described earlier, the need for timely execution is, in fact, quite similar.

At the other end of the spectrum of packaged trades (the upper left-hand corner of Figure 4-3), there are what we have arbitrarily labeled "slow packaged trades." Consider, for example, a value-oriented market timer who buys a slice of the general stock market because stocks are "cheap." Or, consider a value-oriented money manager who sells consumer nondurable companies on the conviction that their price has been driven too high by others and swaps them for a package of international oils on the ground that their price has been driven too low. Clearly, these trades are very insensitive to time and are based solely upon price. Moreover, because they *are* based solely upon price, they could easily benefit from a patient market approach; the buyer might alter the names of the particular "buys" according to price so that only the cheapest stocks are selected, one might employ other forms of creative long-term, price-sensitive tactics.

A complex variety of possible trading strategies are suggested by Figure 4-3; how potential traders signal their presence and intentions is another important dimension of the typology. A large trader with no information advantage does not want to be mistaken for an information-laden trader because this may precipitate an unwanted response from other market participants. And a large, patient trader focusing on cheapness does not want to be mistaken for an impatient trader. The tactics and techniques of different trading strategies are crucial elements of these signalling problems.

DERIVATIVE SECURITIES AND THE MARKET FOR MACRO DECISIONS

Another quite separate but important recent development is the growth of derivative securities, including particularly the growth in both equity index futures (for example, the Standard & Poor's 500 Index future) and equity index options. Originally developed primarily as hedging vehicles, these derivative securities were actively traded by brokers, individuals, and others in the first several years after their introduction, but they were rarely traded by pension funds or their external managers. Recently, however, large innovative institutional owners have begun to use them to implement particular asset allocation strategies, including some emerging forms of dynamic risk management.

As an example of this, consider again our plan sponsor with an equity portfolio structured as in Figure 4-2 (i.e., a collection of specialist, active managers augmented with a passive portion, such as an index or completeness fund). Suppose that the sponsor wants considerable exposure to equities because he expects equities to earn the highest real rate of return over long periods of time. Further suppose, however, that the sponsor is very concerned about the substantial short-term volatility of equities and hence seeks an asset allocation policy that provides downside protection over, say, a calendar year. To achieve such a goal in any given year, the sponsor can adopt a dynamic strategy that decreases portfolio risk as equities fall and increases its risk as equities rise. Such dynamic asset allocation strategies, which at each point in time determine the amount put at risk according to the criterion of how much the sponsor can afford to lose, are commonly known as "portfolio protection" or "portfolio insurance" strategies.

There are a variety of ways to implement a program of portfolio insurance, but they all require the sale of stocks as the stock market falls. In particular, formula-triggered approaches have recently been developed that closely approximate insurance in its purest form; that is, they attempt to produce the same outcome as that which can be achieved with the purchase of a put option on an equity portfolio.[9] While the formula-triggered approaches work remarkably well, they do require frequent (perhaps weekly) trading, albeit in "small" amounts.[10] This presents a problem for our sponsor who has multiple equity managers because he now has to frequently sell off or buy a slice of each manager's portfolio. Such actions can be confusing for the specialty managers and can dysfunctionally interfere with their decision-making and trading processes. A more practical solution is to buy and sell stock index futures to implement the dynamic strategy. This use of futures leads to approximately the same risk posture as the alternative of transacting in the underlying securities, but allows the sponsor to overlay a risk management strategy on top of a carefully designed system of multiple specialists without interfering in their stock-picking decisions. Indeed, it can be (and sometimes is) done without their knowledge. Thus, much like a completeness fund, the use of futures for portfolio insurance separates the function of centralized risk management from that of active stock selection. Risk management in this form can thus be implemented by yet another specialist or by the in-house pension staff in a manner completely decoupled from the operations and strategies of the other specialists on the team.[11]

Index futures can be used for many purposes other than the portfolio insurance example described above. Internal pension staffs and external money managers can use them in most macro decisions, such as aggressive market-timing decisions, or hedges against unwanted risks that can arise in implementing various trading strategies. Moreover, the futures trading by pension funds and other large institutional owners is only a small fraction of the futures trading that takes place today. Broker-dealers use them extensively to hedge their own trading positions. Investors of all sorts use them for both hedging market risks and placing speculative market bets. Arbitrageurs use them for implementing a wide variety of arbitrage strategies. Today, the total trading volume in the futures markets substantially exceeds the trading volume in the underlying stocks in the NYSE. Indeed, the futures markets have become *the* markets for macro financial decisions; they are the most convenient and efficient markets for implementing these decisions; the observed trading volume is greater; and the prices probably represent the best single indication of the prospective price at which macro decisions can truly be implemented.

Of course, there is a strong linkage between the macro market for index futures and options (i.e., packages) and the micro market for individual stocks. When any future is trading at a price out of line with the micro market (that is, the current market prices for its constituent stocks, adjusted for the differences in carrying cost), there is a classic arbitrage opportunity to buy in one market and sell in the substitute market. For example, if the future is overpriced relative to the stocks in the index itself, the arbitrage involves buying the stocks in the index (or a close substitute) via a program trade and selling the future against this position. In a fully competitive market, the prices in the macro and micro markets should thus differ by no more than the execution cost of one of these "index program trades."[12] In practice, this linkage between the markets is kept fairly tight by the arbitraging activities of such participants as broker-dealers (who trade for their own account), corporate cash managers (who purchase the "synthetic money market securities" created by such arbitrage opportunities), and institutional investors (who want, for example, to take a long position in equities and do so in the cheaper of the two markets).

The linkages among various markets can be illustrated by the following vignette that portrays a recent, hypothetical trading day on Wall Street. In the morning there is news of an unexpected rebound in oil prices that dampens the outlook for continued low inflation; this, in turn, leads to expectations of higher interest rates. Bond prices tumble. In sympathy, speculators soon turn bearish on stocks, too. Of course, the cheapest and most efficient way to bet against stocks in general is to sell index futures. When this occurs, the prices of these futures tumble and open a "gap" between futures prices and the apparent prices of individual stocks. Attracted by this opportunity, arbitrageurs buy futures and sell stocks (possibly selling them short) in index program trades; this drives individual stock prices down. Very late in the trading session, the portfolio insurers (described earlier) recalculate their desired equity positions on the basis of the now-lower stock prices and conclude that they should own fewer equities. Rather than wait until the next morning, they sell in the futures market a half-hour before the close.[13] Again the futures prices fall relative to the apparent prices of the underlying stocks and open another opportunity for the arbitrageurs. The arbitrageurs again buy futures and sell index program trades to exploit the opportunity. By the close of the market, the cumulative impact of these activities has pushed the Dow Jones average down by 35 points.

In the newspapers the next day, the sharp market decline is blamed on the program traders. Blaming the market drop on the program traders, however, is a bit like blaming the floor for the shattering of a dropped egg. What has really happened is that index futures (and related options) have now made it much easier for both aggressive investors (the speculators) and conservative investors (the portfolio insurers) to implement quick and sizable changes in their effective asset allocation. The sporadic short-term interplay of these quick and sizable shifts appears to have caused an increase in the very short-term (hourly and intraday) volatility of market prices. This "volatility" originates in the macro markets and is transferred to the market prices for individual stocks by the index program traders.[14] In a sense, markets have become much more responsive to investors' short-term hopes and fears because of the development of a cheap and efficient market for macro decisions and macro trades.[15]

Looking toward the future, as the number of available equity index futures continues to proliferate, it will allow investors to bet or hedge on dimensions of risk other than just the market risk represented by the S&P 500. Even today, for example, one can hold futures or options positions on the Major Market Index, the S&P 100, the S&P 500, the NYSE Composite Index, the Value Line Index (small stocks), high-beta stocks, technology stocks, computer stocks, oil stocks, airline stocks and others. Additional futures and options, defined over particular industries, sectors, or various other characteristics, are clearly on the way. These derivative securities will form the vehicles for an intermediate market, halfway between the macro market for very broad decisions and the micro market for individual stocks. In theory, for example, one can imagine a future corporate pension plan sponsor managing its entire pension fund in-house by avoiding individual stocks and instead substituting these intermediate-market vehicles; but it is more likely that these intermediate-market vehicles will allow pension sponsors to implement more easily and more cheaply the control of central risk management and investment policy direction that they have already staked out as their responsibility. In addition, they will give money managers and individual traders the ability to place bets at the intermediate level of industries or other equity characteristics more conveniently than is now possible. Finally, of course, the opportunities for creative arbitrage will grow geometrically as the program traders equilibrate the relative pricing in the micro, macro, and intermediate markets.

Anticipating the future, many large institutional owners are also becoming more actively interested in international diversification. While the percentage of foreign stocks held in pension funds is still quite small (perhaps several percent), the recent growth in this sector has been rapid. As this growth continues, the country in which a company is headquartered (and the currency in which its stock is traded) will become another important overlay of the investment decision process. It will no longer just be stocks versus bonds, but German stocks versus U.S. stocks versus Australian bonds. And futures will play an important role here, too. Already, there are currency futures and stock index futures for the major world equity markets. In the current early phases of this international diversification, the external money managers are playing the role of country allocators. But it is clear that this international decision making will evolve in much the same manner as domestic decision making; country and currency factors will become important components of the macro decision making that is formulated and carried out at the corporate sponsor level. As this happens, it will enrich the dimensions of the macro decision process by offering new possibilities for both risk management and active asset allocation.

PRIVATE SECTOR IMPLICATIONS

As we have seen, the growing concentration of financial ownership in a relatively small number of large institutional hands has been one of several important influences on the evolution of decision making and trading in U.S. financial markets.

This evolution is perhaps best typified by the evolution of large, corporate pension funds. Long-term relationships with well-established, low-turnover investment management institutions that handled all aspects of investment decision making have been replaced by more complex hierarchical organizations that span traditional organizational boundaries. In-house pension committees, in-house pension staffs, and an entirely new pension-consulting industry have developed to shepherd the growing accumulations of pension wealth. These internal decision-making units have been charged with allocating the pension assets in the broadest sense and with actively managing a portfolio of active and passive external money managers. The macro decisions of these in-house staffs have become an important element affecting markets and market prices. A passive money management industry has sprung up to satisfy the plan sponsors' needs for low-cost diversification. The active external money managers have adapted to these new business realities and to the opportunities stemming from improved technology by proliferating in number and differentiating their investment approaches into more and more specialized and distinct approaches to active stock selection.[16]

As a result of the new, active approaches to macro management undertaken by the corporations themselves and the pressures for performance created in the money management business, institutional turnover rates and the size of stock transactions have climbed dramatically. In a world of unfixed commissions, the management of the price impacts of these greater transaction demands has become essential, and the pressures for such management have created an era of creativity and experimentation in new trading strategies and tactics.

At the same time, the futures, options, and other derivative security markets have expanded rapidly and have opened new opportunities for risk management (and perhaps speculation) at the macro level of investment decision making. These derivative securities have become important vehicles of the macro market in which macro traders implement their decisions most conveniently and most cheaply. As we indicated earlier, it seems certain that whole new families of money management products, futures, and other derivative securities defined over industries and sectors and countries, with their own traders and their own prices, will evolve to formalize an "intermediate market" for investment decision making.

This evolution in investment decision making brings important opportunities and serious challenges for the corporate pension plan sponsor and other large institutional owners. In thinking through the role of the pension fund in the sponsoring firm's overall financial strategy and its responsibility to meet the needs of beneficiaries, lenders, and shareholders, the sponsoring firm's management must periodically reconsider the different macro decisions that determine the fund's long-run returns. They can choose from a variety of different defensive risk-management techniques as well as aggressive asset-allocation roles. They must continually sharpen their ability to evaluate specialized money managers and their trading tactics. And they can only have confidence in their ability to do all of these tasks if they can maintain a new and sophisticated level of in-house investment expertise and judgment. For these sponsors, an overriding current problem is the nurturing of the requisite decision-making skills within corporate environments where cultures and pay scales are often a world apart from those of the outside money management industry.

At the same time, this evolution has also created real problems for some of the large traditional investment managers who once dominated the pension business. On the one hand, their overall investment counseling role has been usurped by the sponsors' in-house staffs; and on the other hand, they have found it increasingly difficult to compete with the legions of new small firms in the high-fee, value-added segments of the specialized equity management business. For them, the challenge is to marshal their considerable people and money resources so as to formulate distinctive new money management approaches in which their resources provide a credible competitive advantage. One approach is to redefine their role as a specialist in many of the centralized macro decisions that pension funds face and reclaim their position as the pension fund's single most important investment counselor.

At first glance, the surge in turnover that has accompanied this institutional evolution might appear to be a bonanza for the institutional broker-dealers on Wall Street. But the high volume has been offset by dramatically shrinking commissions and margins. Interestingly, the market for transaction services has also become increasingly differentiated as investment decision makers have created new trading strategies in the micro market, the macro market, and across the two sectors. Importantly, one of the largest of the new segments—program trading—requires access to broadly based market information, substantial order flow, and capital; it is a segment where the largest and best capitalized of the brokers can wield a substantial competitive advantage. For the somewhat smaller (though still large) firms, it is tempting to believe that one can segment today's more differentiated trading market and compete in only selected segments. But that is a difficult strategy to implement successfully in the trading business. There are, it turns out, clear economies of scale across all segments, because increased order flow from different traders with different needs makes any particular broker-dealer firm a tougher competitor in all segments. There are real questions for the institutional broker-dealers to ask: Can we afford *not* to compete in program trading? In futures trading? In arbitrage trading? In block trading? And, if we cannot afford *not* to compete, where can we get the capital and how can we build the critical mass of order flow necessary to compete?

Other issues have also emerged for broker-dealers in the new world of more differentiated trading. The dual character of order flows in the macro and micro markets have created many more opportunities for firms to trade profitably for their own account. As these opportunities proliferate, clients will begin to demand a share of these trading profits by, in effect, extracting a rent for certain types of order flow. At the same time, aggressive trading by broker-dealers for their own account has begun to call into question the meaning of the word service. Trading firms must thus learn to organize their portfolios of trading businesses so as to minimize the growing conflicts of interest between their own and their clients' needs and still use their capital profitability, for commissions are unlikely to be a sufficient reward in the future.

PUBLIC POLICY IMPLICATIONS

The outlook for the structure of markets, including questions relating to the future structure and viability of the New York Stock Exchange, is murkier. Prior to the advent of program and macro trading in its current form, there had been (and today there still is) much talk of the imminent demise of the NYSE. With the growing dominance of block trades, the importance of the exchanges as centralized focal points for order flow had clearly diminished. Big trades were being negotiated upstairs and brought to the floor only as a formality to comply with exchange rules. Many observers predicted that there would soon be a dealer-only market, with the dominant players being those with the most capital and the broadest distribution capabilities. The coming advent of worldwide, 24-hour trading has only sharpened the image of the NYSE as a threatened structure.

The growth in program trading, however, has injected a very important burst of many medium-sized orders into the marketplace; and the generally time-sensitive nature of program trading has rejuvenated the need for immediate liquidity in these types of packaged trades. The medium-sized program trades do not necessarily strain any one specialist's capital resources, and centralized order flow clearly serves to aggregate supply and demand information rather than disperse it among a relatively large number of independent dealers. Hence, centralized marketplaces appear best able to satisfy the program traders' particular need for liquidity. Ironically, the growth of macro decisions and resulting program trading may reinforce the need for the very type of centralized future marketplace in which the NYSE could have a clear and perhaps dominant role.

Finally, there has been substantial public concern over the apparent increase in the sudden, pervasive, intraday market updrafts and downwards related to index futures arbitrage. And this concern has sometimes been translated into calls for greater surveillance and regulation of program traders and macro-micro arbitrageurs.[17] Viewed in the context of the evolution of investment decision making, however, a constructive program of regulatory response will be very difficult to formulate. What has really happened is that the focus of decision making has evolved toward macro decisions, and markets have accommodated these changes with the new world of program trading and index futures. To call for important curbs on index-program trading is to fundamentally misunderstand the origins and importance of these new phenomena. Index-program trading is really not the problem; it is merely the vehicle for keeping the macro and micro markets in equilibrium with each other. And it would be almost impossible to turn back the clock and force large institutional owners and investment managers to return to the earlier patterns of investment decision making and trading.

There will, of course, be problems to deal with, and they are likely to be subtle and difficult ones that are hard to assess and remedy. One potential problem, for example, is that the recent development of the index futures markets may encourage greater numbers of investors to adopt short-term asset allocation tactics (such as portfolio insurance) based upon risk reduction, speculative market timing, or both. These tactics are likely to exacerbate any future market volatility. Ultimately, it could be that the development of these large and active macro markets will lead to higher market peaks and deeper market troughs.

Another problem is that the evolution of the macro markets has introduced new and different types of short-term "market" information, as well as new ways to profit from them. On any given day, it is valuable to know that a large "program buy" or three large "program sells" are coming, or that portfolio insurance tactics will trigger major program sells at the opening of the next day's market, or that not one of these is going to happen imminently. It is valuable to know when and why the futures indexes are high, relative to the micro markets, and when and why they are sinking rapidly, relative to the micro market. Unfortunately, this information is not widely known or widely knowable. The public knows little of this information and, in fact, extremely few market players know it. This suggests an informational inequality that allows "insiders" to profit in ways that are unavailable to, and at the expense of, most investors. Moreover, trading in the micro market can alter prices, and thus profits, on positions in the macro market, and vice versa; this also suggests a potential for subtle but profitable forms of market exploitation and manipulation.

Unfortunately, all of this represents a potential step backward from the idealized view of open, public markets in which the prices are uniform and where all valuable information is widely shared. Equally unfortunate, it is difficult to imagine a general regulatory response that could effectively deal with such knotty concerns that are so inextricably a part of the recent evolution of our markets.

NOTES

1. This chapter describes the prototypical evolution in the national (large) corporate pension market. This same evolution has been occurring, albeit at a substantially reduced pace, in the large public retirement funds and in the medium-sized corporate funds.

2. Immunization involves matching the duration of a fixed-income portfolio to the duration of a client's pension liabilities, and dedication calls for matching all of the future cash inflows and outflows period by period.

3. Passive, in this context, means that trading should not be undertaken on the basis of investment forecasts, though this might be done if it serves changing client needs.

4. See *Pensions and Investment Age* (May 1986).

5. Many of these recent new firms were formed, of course, by individuals and small groups leaving large firms, articulating a distinctive investment approach, hanging out a shingle, and doubling their fee structure. Indeed, it could be argued that many of the large active money management organizations have really been worth much more dead than alive (that is, their people have been worth more repackaged into smaller organizations).

6. Interestingly, the mutual fund business has begun to evolve in much the same way as the large pension market: there has been enormous growth in mutual fund assets in the last several years, with much of this money flowing into a new generation of specialty funds. And the proliferation of these funds has led to a mini-industry of market letters and retail brokers that offer advice on what to "buy" and "sell." While the bulk of these changes have been rooted in consumer-marketing strategies and the economics of retail distribution, a significant thrust has come once again from the pension system through the demands created by the growth in self-directed retirement plans (e.g., IRA, Keogh and 401(k) plans). Moreover, the differentiated investment processes needed to manage all of the new and specialized funds reinforces the differentiation and specialization occurring in the large pension market, and vice versa.

7. For an interesting discussion of this interplay, see Jack L. Treynor, "Implementation of Strategy: Execution" in *Managing Investment Portfolios*, John Maginn and Donald Tuttle, eds. (Boston: Warren, Gorham, and Lamont, 1983).

8. The brokers are only transitory market makers; they temporarily position a security until they can find a buyer.

9. The direct purchase of a put option is generally not a viable alternative; usually there is no market for put options of one year (or more) on stock indexes. Furthermore, the investor usually wants to "insure" a unique portfolio that is quite dissimilar from one of the common stock indexes.

10. Amounts that are small in terms of total assets; the trades are not necessarily small in dollar amounts.

11. Portfolio insurance, in its precise, formula-driven form, is a burgeoning industry with something like $20–25 billion of equities being "insured" with futures-related programs executed by advisory firms. While this number is a small fraction of all institutionally owned equities, it has grown in only a few years. In addition, there is probably a substantial body of assets managed implicitly in this way—though without the explicit quantitative formulas of formal portfolio-insurance approaches.

12. This is really just a very particular form of program trade; namely, one that is executed immediately in the stocks of an index. The Major Markets Index is the one most often used today in this arbitrage game. When the popular press writes about "program trading" it is often this very particular form to which they are referring. See, for example: "Those Big Swings on Wall Street: A Complex Game Called Program Trading," *Business Week*, April 7, 1986, pp. 32–36.

13. Note that portfolio-insurance-related trading is destabilizing for the market as a whole. While the insurees limit their own risk by such tactics, their trading activity tends to magnify the fluctuations in market prices. There is, thus, a potential danger for the market as a whole in the growth of portfolio-insurance strategies.

14. Actually, the volatility of stock prices (as measured, for example, by the standard deviation of daily or weekly stock price changes) has not really increased at all, and in fact, it has actually decreased a bit from some earlier years. What has increased, however, is the frequency of sharp, sudden, pervasive updrafts and downdrafts, across virtually all of the large-capitalization stocks in the futures indexes, caused by these trading practices. To the careful analyst who trades on fundamentals and has just recently purchased GM after an exhaustive investigation, the sharp $2 drop in GM's price triggered by some unknown program trader sure feels like increased volatility.

15. An extreme form of this short-term volatility can occur just before the market's close on futures- and options-expiration dates. On these dates the futures and options traders with

established arbitrage positions become extremely sensitive to time (they need to liquidate their positions *at the close*) and quite insensitive to price. Because this extreme volatility is such a special case, we do not dwell upon it here, though popular accounts of program trading often focus upon it.

16. It would be misleading to imply that all large corporate pension funds have embarked upon all (or any) of the changes and strategies discussed in this chapter. In fact, quite a number of institutional pools are still managed in "the old way," and several of the new techniques are only now being adopted by a sizable number of funds. Nonetheless, this evolution does generally characterize many large funds and is clearly the leading edge of change in the pension-fund industry. Moreover, medium-sized corporate funds and large public retirement systems are now beginning to follow. It seems clear that this evolution has substantial momentum and will continue to change the ways in which the large institutional owners affect the financial markets.

17. Some observers have argued that the public's uneasiness with these new phenomena is one of the reasons that individual investors have been liquidating their direct equity holdings and rechanneling some of the proceeds into equity mutual funds.

FIVE

UNDERWRITING REGULATION AND THE SHELF REGISTRATION PHENOMENON

Joseph Auerbach and Samuel L. Hayes, III

Earlier chapters have chronicled how, in the years since the reform legislation of the 1930s brought them under regulatory control, the U.S. securities markets have undergone a profound transformation. As a result of the post–World War II economic expansion and the subsequent economic dislocations of the 1970s and early 1980s, arrangements for raising new capital, in particular, have undergone considerable modification. This chapter examines this process of change through the prism of the securities underwriting function; we explore the counterpoint of the regulatory framework, on the one hand, and the evolving capital market forces on the other. Our study examines the new patterns created when regulatory constraints are loosened to accommodate the competitive forces in the marketplace.

As a case in point, we focus on the recent introduction of "shelf registration." This procedure, adopted by the Securities and Exchange Commission in its Rule 415 under the Securities Act of 1933, permits certain capital issuers who register for public sale a block of new securities (as required by the 1933 act) to put them "on the shelf" for up to two years so as to time their sale to the most favorable selling opportunities that arise during those two years. In the course of this presentation, we will raise questions about the extent to which the arrangements governing this important contemporary financing option are congruent with the aims of the original legislation and the extent to which those legislative aims are still appropriate in the 1980s.

The period of our analysis begins even before the 1930s, as we examine the circumstances and forces that led to the passage of the original reform legislation in this area of capital market activity; then we study subsequent changes in the environment that underlie the contemporary shelf registration procedure.

PRE–1930 SECURITIES MARKETS

To comprehend the foundations of contemporary securities-underwriting arrangements in the United States, it is important to understand the economic and political events that led up to the Great Depression and ultimately precipitated the reform legislation that has now been sustained for more than a half-century. For by 1933, the bitter facts of economic collapse had become inextricably linked in the public mind with the market crash of 1929 and, more broadly, with the increasingly feverish operations of high finance during the 1920s.

MARKET ENVIRONMENT

As the industrial momentum of the United States had grown, so the size and scope of its business and national governmental sectors had grown as well. The merger wave of 1889–1902 brought with it a consolidation of what had in many instances been fragmented local or regional industries. This consolidation was fostered initially by the spanning of the continent by the railroads and the telegraph; and in the 1920s, by the radio which ushered in the age of national marketing.

While this national industrial consolidation was taking place, the number and size of incorporated businesses also grew, reflecting the expanding economy characteristic of much of this period. Although more than half of the growth in corporate assets was consistently accomplished through internal depreciation set-asides and retention of profits,[1] a substantial part of the acquired assets was derived from external borrowing (both short- and long-term) and, particularly during the late 1920s, from the issuance of new equity securities.[2]

Both the domestic and the foreign financing demands of the government sector also grew. Prior to 1900, the United States had been a net importer of capital, but by the end of World War I the country had become a capital exporter.

The size and composition of the domestic U.S. investor community was itself changing and expanding. Prior to World War I, wealthy individuals had been the most important source of both debt and equity capital, but subsequent changes in the tax law reduced their importance. Then, because of the small amount of institutionalized savings, intermediaries were forced to turn to a new source of funds—the individual investors of modest means who entered the public markets in the early twentieth century. It is likely that the Liberty Bond sales campaigns during World War I initially helped make these individuals comfortable with the notion of putting their money into the securities markets. While statistics show that individuals at first invested more heavily in debt than in equity securities, by 1927 they had shifted to corporate equities.[3] By the end of the 1920s, the holdings of individual investors constituted the overwhelming majority of public equity securities and about 50 percent of public debt securities.

A variety of banking intermediaries competed for this growing volume of financing business. The historically dominant private banks remained noteworthy, but they were increasingly joined by the U.S. commercial banks; these grew rapidly in total assets as they underwent a consolidation that by 1933 had reduced the total number of individual banks by half.[4]

SYNDICATIONS

Continuing throughout the latter part of the nineteenth century and almost through the end of World War I, the volume of savings available for investment had proved inadequate to meet the expanding demands of business enterprise for new capital. As a consequence, a considerable period of time (up to two years) usually elapsed between the first offering of an issue and the final disposition of these securities to the investing public.[5] Thus it can be argued that prior to 1920 the United States had in fact engaged in a historical era of de facto "shelf" securities offerings.

After the end of World War I, the greater availability of capital made possible a more rapid process of securities flotation. At the same time, however, the syndicate operations that in the years before the war had been responsive to the paucity of capital now faced the challenge of adapting to quite different circumstances. In practice, syndicates felt compelled to make themselves larger (in order to distribute the heightened risks of long flotations), simpler (in order to pass risks along more quickly), and faster acting (in order to try to reduce risks altogether). Adding to the force of these changes were the competitive circumstances of many of the investment houses themselves. Although the more-established issuing houses received ample requests for their services, the newer or smaller firms that sought to break into the business or to move up within the industry's pyramidal structure could do so only by tapping pockets of supply and demand not already buttoned up.

These developments did much to alter the way the industry worked. In the first place, as syndicates grew larger, they also became more streamlined; their traditional organization as a portfolio of different functional groups began to give way to a simpler, twofold division into underwriting and selling groups. Second, as fees for underwriting services declined, it became increasingly attractive for the underwriters themselves to become more extensively involved than they had been in distribution, either directly or through affiliated organizations. Third, as the smaller individual investors became the dominant buying force in the market (particularly for equities), high-powered sales techniques were rapidly developed to reach them. Finally, as demand fed on itself and created even greater demand, investment houses began to face the constant challenge of finding enough products to sell. By the time of the reform legislation of the 1930s, industry practice appeared to be driven less by a desire to make a fair profit from underwriting and distributing sound, well-researched securities to the public than by a need to keep the securities pipeline full.

DISSEMINATING CREDIT INFORMATION

In no small measure, the complex relationships among originators, underwriters, and distributors that had long characterized the work of investment banking syndicates depended on the trust that syndicate members felt for the research and judgment of the originating house. Since it was far too expensive for each syndicate participant to do its own analysis of a security's underlying value, they regularly agreed to the extra fees for management services that the originating houses demanded. During the 1920s, however, as participants found themselves handling ever larger volumes of securities, they often put more pressure on the syndicate manager's ability to generate and disseminate information than he was able to bear. This was both unintentional and undesired, but it followed directly from the participants' urgent calls for more products to sell.

While the syndicate members depended heavily on syndicate managers for investigations and services, syndicates were usually in no position to discipline managers for shortfalls in issuer investigation or other activities related to an offering. Instead, these prestigious houses continued to use their commanding position in the industry (and at the apex of individual syndicate pyramids) to dictate the terms of participation. Thus, if a smaller house wanted to be included in future syndications, it had little choice but to accept the opportunities and terms that were offered by the originating firms on current securities offerings.

The boom in equity financing during the latter half of the 1920s made the problem even worse. Stock offerings that required a new kind of information based upon a specific corporation's operations, rather than upon the identification of a risk class of fixed-income securities, appeared; and this new situation underscored the existing chaos in accounting principles and practices, the inadequacy of the listing requirements on all major exchanges, and the gross lack of comparability among corporate balance sheets and income statements. Much to the detriment of public investors, a true "information gap" developed as accurate and timely information became (by the 1920s) more crucial than ever before. But traditional business practice, exacerbated by the competitive circumstances of the time, made the distribution of such information impossible, and the great crash of 1929 produced a special crisis of legitimacy. Afterward, neither the confidence nor the faith upon which legitimacy rests could be restored by simple acts of belief; better information was required, but it was not forthcoming.

LEGISLATIVE HISTORY

Thus, by the 1930s, the country had lost confidence in the financial system and in the people who led it. The national election campaign of 1932 questioned the legitimacy not only of banks but of the entire financial system. The national political leadership promised to "fix" the myriad financial ills that beset the current system. Following the 1932 election, the legislative agenda sought to devise a system that (unlike such earlier quasi-judicial regulatory models as the one created by the Interstate Commerce Act, which had already been in force for nearly fifty years) would effectively eliminate these abuses on a self-regulatory basis.

One consequence was the Glass-Steagall Act, which, in 1933, separated "commercial banking" (deposit-taking and loan-extension activities) from investment banking (activities principally related to the corporate securities business). In addition, the Securities Act of 1933 sought to expose the inner workings of the securities-issuance procedure to intense public scrutiny by compelling the disclosure of material information about new securities. The securities-issuance industry would be regulated not by breaking it up, or by promising to safeguard investors against the inevitable risks of capitalist enterprise, but by forcing it to disclose relevant information. Congress believed that this combination of "regulation by prohibition" (the Glass-Steagall Act) and "regulation by information" (the Securities Act of 1933) would achieve a comprehensive overhaul of the procedures for the public issuance of securities; thus it would restore economic vitality to, and public support for, the capital-raising mechanism.

It is important to note, however, that the framers of the 1933 act were not addressing a previously unknown set of difficulties that were suddenly thrust upon an investing public by the happenstance of a great economic crisis. Instead, legislators were—and consciously felt themselves to be—grappling with a thorny collection of issues that had been plaguing legislators and regulators since before the turn of the century. In no small measure, their allegiance to the idea of a federal regulatory effort, based on the principle of information dissemination, grew out of their convictions about how and why past efforts had failed.

What they saw was a crazy quilt of blue-sky legislation, at the state level, that had emerged from a morass of legal theory, parochial interest, and administrative practice. Previous efforts at regulation and coordination at the national level—an interstate approach—had also been unsuccessful; trade groups such as the Investment Bankers Association had made initial efforts at policing but had then backed off. The New York Stock Exchange and other exchanges (themselves dominated by their securities-dealer members), to which the states had allowed an immense and unprecedented grant of de facto authority to regulate securities in the public interest, had consistently dragged their feet on reform.

The framers of the 1933 Securities Act confronted not only this history of institutional failure and legislative neglect, but also the political realities of the emerging New Deal. In his speech accepting the Democratic party nomination, Franklin Roosevelt promised to pursue a strategy of "letting in the light."[6] Influenced by the thinking of Louis Brandeis and his followers, Roosevelt saw a genuine threat to private property in the power of the small group of financial interests that was dominating the nation's economy and manipulating the value of securities in the stock market. During his August 20, 1932, speech at Columbus, Ohio, for example, FDR called upon the government to "counterbalance this power" and "protect private property from ruthless manipulation in the stock market and corporate system."[7] For Roosevelt, then, there was little doubt that the federal government could play a significant role in regulating both the public issuance of securities and the securities-trading markets— a role designed to offset the exercise of economic power concentrated in private hands.

Roosevelt drew the line, however, against more extensive government action. Washington could not, and should not, try to guarantee the soundness of individual investment decisions or safeguard investors against the possibility of loss. What it *could* do was give potential investors access to all material information before they reached an investment decision.

STRUCTURE OF THE LEGISLATION

In essence, the Securities Act of 1933 directed that when an issuer or related agency sold securities, the sale had to be accompanied by a publicly filed sales document (a prospectus) laying out, in accordance with government specifications, all of the information deemed material to an investor's decision to purchase. The act also established civil liabilities for sales documents that proved to be inadequate or misleading.

In all events, the issuer itself was unconditionally liable under

Section 11 of the 1933 act for any misstatement or material omission. Furthermore, the securities underwriters were conditionally liable unless it could be shown that they had exercised necessary care in their own independent review of the sales material's disclosures; that is, that they had conducted a "reasonable investigation." This protection from liability or penalty for those underwriters who could demonstrate a "reasonable investigation" became known colloquially as the "due diligence" provision.

Significantly, the 1933 Securities Act rejected the concept, contained in a number of the blue-sky laws of various states, that required a public agency to pass on the *quality* of the security or its issuer. Rather, the act's requirements were limited to ensuring a thorough exposure of all facts material to an investment decision; the investor was left to draw appropriate conclusions.

In 1934, Congress passed the Securities Exchange Act, which in addition to creating the Securities and Exchange Commission (SEC), declared that securities transactions (on exchanges and over-the-counter) affected the public interest. The act also regulated and controlled pertinent trading practices, including transactions by insiders, required the filing of appropriate reports and proxy statements, and attempted to ensure "fair and honest markets."

By 1934, then, the United States had put in place its legislative response to the perceived abuses of the pre–depression era. Now the stage was set for testing the viability of these new rules in the subsequent economic and financial-market environments.

THE POST–WORLD WAR II MARKETPLACE

At the end of World War II, following the period of extraordinary conditions in the financial markets during the war, American securities markets and their servicing intermediaries returned to a normalized condition. The impressive peacetime growth in real GNP and in accompanying savings rates was reflected in a rising stock market, leading to an accumulation of wealth among individuals. This period, however, also saw the initiation and growth of institutional pools of capital, which were principally centered around insurance companies, pension funds, and mutual funds. Economic growth spurred an increasing appetite for new external financings by U.S. corporations. New external financings rose from $4.2 billion to $8.1 billion over the decade ending in 1959.[8] Furthermore, reliance on debt (as opposed to equity) financings grew markedly, particularly during the 1960s.[9]

As external capital raising accelerated and as the size and the influence of institutional investors increased, the character of both the primary and secondary securities markets changed. First, a larger supply of securities appeared in the hands of professional portfolio managers who demanded realistic pricing and who kept secondary markets active. The ranks of research analysts also grew as intermediaries sought to better serve the professional portfolio manager's needs. Information, in turn, increased in quantity and quality, as it was required to support the increased trading of securities in the secondary markets.

These financial market developments also affected the manner in which the reform regulations of the 1930s were administered, particularly in the cases of the Securities Act of 1933 and the Securities Exchange Act of 1934, since both acts required disclosing information to investors. When these acts were passed, neither contained disclosure requirements deemed to be *functionally* related. The disclosure requirement of the Securities Act, for example, was designed only to prevent fraud in the sale of new securities offered to the public—a transactional concept—while in the Securities Exchange Act of 1934, the disclosure requirement was linked to a regulatory concept involving criminal penalties as part of a broad attack on securities fraud, insider trading, "excessive speculation," and "manipulation and control." The regulatory pattern in the 1934 act, while also relying on information as the medium, sought to ensure, through required periodic and episodic reporting, that material information would enter the public domain under a system backed up by penalties and sanctions. Thus, a buyer or seller of securities would have ready access to pertinent information that made it possible to reach an informed opinion regarding the value of those securities, either directly or through the advice of others.

In 1967 the SEC took its first formal step toward integrating the requirements of the two acts—a move first suggested in a seminal article by Milton Cohen, a prominent securities law-yer.[10] Under the 1933 act, the SEC adopted a simplified registra-tion form (Form S-7) for securities offered for cash by issuers having long records of earnings and stability of management and subject to the reporting requirements of the 1934 act.

Concurrently, the SEC appointed an internal study group to examine disclosure systems in detail. The resulting 1969 report, "Disclosure to Investors: Reappraisal of Administrative Policies under the 1933 and 1934 Acts" (known as the Wheat Report), contained extensive recommendations in three areas: the con-ceptual strengthening and improvement of reporting under the 1934 act, the administration and enforcement of preparation and filing, and the dissemination of the information being re-ported.[11]

Consistent with the Wheat Report, the SEC supplemented its initial move by adopting Form S-16 in 1970. This action per-mitted issuers who were qualified to use Form S-7 when regis-tering securities (under the 1933 act) for sale in certain second-ary distributions to incorporate, by reference only, information already filed in 1934 act reports. This broadening of the nature of disclosure assumed that, since the issuer had similar securities currently outstanding, the market price already reflected the information upon which a secondary distribution would neces-sarily be based. Eligibility for Form S-7, which was limited to a relatively small group of issuers, remained the test for this significant step toward integration of disclosure.

The SEC's decision to proceed in this fashion was almost certainly influenced by the rapidly accumulating academic re-search and literature that provided the empirical evidence of the financial markets' efficient valuation of securities. The efficient market concept had become both the reason for requiring broadened disclosure under the 1934 act and the justification for considering those disclosures sufficient to meet the requirements of the 1933 act; thus it ultimately led to the authorization of shelf registration.

In essence, the efficient market hypothesis states that, at any point in time, the market price of a security fully reflects all available information about that security.[12] The average inves-tor need not, therefore, be aware of any particular piece of information in order to be able to participate in the market on a fair basis with other investors, even those investors with greater sophistication or better means of collecting and analyzing data about individual companies. At any particular time (according to the theory), the "true" value of a security is as likely to be above the actual market price as below it. Therefore, every buyer or seller of that security (other than one who possesses inside information) is in exactly the same position. The strongest adherents of the theory would maintain, furthermore, that not even an investor possessed of specific, undisclosed information about a company could identify an undervalued or overpriced security, because the implications of that information would already have been reflected in the security's market price.[13]

In 1976, satisfied that improvement had been realized in the quality, scope, and dissemination of those 1934 act reports upon which the Wheat Report recommendations had been premised, the SEC broadened the availability of Form S-7 to primary securities; that is, the form was made available to new securities issuers. In all, both the range of the eligible issuers and the transactions for which it was available were enlarged.[14] An Advisory Committee on Corporate Disclosure was appointed by the SEC to study the issues further; in 1977, it recommended a complete integration of the two disclosure systems. The advisory committee's report also led the SEC, in 1978, to enlarge the availability of its registration form (which previously had been restricted to secondary offerings of outstanding securities) to include primary offerings as well. These recommendations of the advisory committee were fully incorporated in March 1982, when the SEC adopted an integrated disclosure system that comprehensively restructured the reporting requirements under both the 1933 and 1934 acts. A three-tier registration structure involving Forms S-1, S-2, and S-3 was adopted under the 1933 act, with issuer eligibility dependent upon the presumed degree of availability of information about the registrant in the public domain. The basis of classification was to be the registrant's participation in the disclosure and reporting system under the 1934 act.[15]

Having adopted its integrated disclosure system, the SEC now became receptive to implementation of a rule designed to accelerate to the ultimate degree—a matter of hours or even minutes—the incubation period between the registration of a new security (fixed at twenty days under the 1933 act) and its public offering. The regulatory stage was thus set for the introduction of shelf registration.[16]

In adopting integrated disclosure, the SEC specifically recognized its essential significance to a system of accelerated securities issuance; this realization was the rationale for shelf registrations. Integrated disclosure, in the SEC's view, represents a particularly valuable ingredient in market efficiency. It has been said that under Rule 415 companies for which Form S-3 is available "provide a steady stream of high quality information to the marketplace (which) is constantly digested and synthesized by financial analysts, who act as essential conduits, and is broadly disseminated on a timely basis."[17]

INTRODUCTION OF SHELF REGISTRATION

Developments within the U.S. economy and within the securities markets themselves provided an important impetus to the evolution in regulatory oversight and the ultimate introduction of shelf registrations. The growing sophistication of corporate financial officers, the institutionalization of the savings and investment industries, the increasingly broad and deep secondary markets for securities, and the growing links between the U.S. financial sector and the Euromarkets (as well as other important national markets) were all significant determining factors. These developments put greater pressure on underwriting spreads (the difference between the underwriter's cost for a security and its publicly announced selling price). More and more, institutional investors were being granted discounts on their new offerings, often through "overtrading," or the practice of receiving artificially high prices, on a yield basis, for portfolio holdings in swap for new securities.

Corporate clients were coming to view term loans from commercial banks, Euromarket financings made outside the United States (in either dollar or foreign currency), and interest rate and currency swaps as trade-offs for conventional U.S. debt placements. They have increasingly opted for these offshore and swap arrangements, not only to realize a lower average net cost of funds, but also because the speedier execution of private or offshore transactions outside the requirements of the 1933 act enables them to take advantage of temporary windows of opportunity in various of the world's capital markets.

In response, a conviction was developing within the issuer and regulatory communities that the procedures for issuing securities in the United States should be streamlined, particularly for large, well-known, frequent capital raisers. Moves in this direction, it was hoped, would reduce bureaucratic delays and lower the overall issuance costs for corporate capital raisers. Many observers expected that throwing open the capital-raising activity to de facto competitive bidding would increase the number of underwriting competitors and enhance the attraction of domestic financings (vis-à-vis alternatives available in Euromarkets, where many of the advantages described already existed).

Under the shelf registration rule, as noted earlier, an eligible issuer is permitted to use its 1933 act registration statement for the offering of a certain maximum amount of a particular class of securities at one or more unspecified points within the succeeding two years. Detailed offering terms are, of course, delayed until the actual commencement of sale. One or more proposed underwriters may also be listed. Within the two-year time limit subsequent to the registration, when the issuer and its advisers see a favorable opportunity in the marketplace, they can quickly effect a sale of some or all of the securities specified in the registration statement. In all likelihood, once the registration statement has been filed, the issuer will from time to time receive calls from various investment banking firms offering to buy the securities at a given set of terms and price; thus, a de facto competitive bidding process emerges.

Similar acquisition procedures were commonly used in the late nineteenth and early twentieth centuries; in the environment of the 1980s, however, because of the higher risks from potential price volatility, underwriters are more loath than they were in earlier times to accept the gradual liquidation of their acquired inventory of securities. Instead, they seek to dispose of it in a matter of hours.

Rule 415 first emerged as a proposal in December 1980, and it was adopted by the SEC in experimental form on March 3, 1982, for a trial period. At the beginning of 1984, shelf registration became a permanent option. Since its introduction, the shelf registration financing technique has made impressive inroads in the U.S. capital markets. To provide a before-and-after perspective, Figure 5-1 shows total annual public financing data for the period since January 1, 1979. (The three years of shelf experience, it will be noted, has also coincided with a record level of public corporate financings.)

As the statistics show, the shelf registration option got off to a fast start and, by the end of 1984, had captured approximately half of the total negotiated-debt market. Penetration of the equity-offering market has been much more modest, reflecting in part the issuers' reluctance to have the prospect of additional earnings dilution overhang the market in anticipation of a later sale of shelf registered securities.

To understand the popularity of the shelf underwriting procedure, one must appreciate the tangible cost savings that have accrued to the issuers. Several studies of comparative all-inclusive (all-in) costs, undertaken by academic researchers under SEC sponsorship, tested this cost-savings hypothesis, and the results did indeed point in the direction of such cost savings.[18] Specifically, the studies suggest that industrial bond issues sold by shelf registration incur an all-in cost of funds between twenty and thirty basis points (portions of one percent, which is one hundred basis points) lower than the all-in cost of funds for comparable nonshelf offerings. The cost savings are apparently achieved because of the more intense bidding by competing underwriters for the bond issues.

The substitution of the shelf format for the earlier, conventional, negotiated underwriting that utilized one of the issuer's traditional investment bankers had been expected to enhance competition; and the evidence of significant, average cost savings for the shelf financings—at least among debt issues—would seem to confirm that this has, in fact, happened.

A closer scrutiny of the actual experience with shelfs indicates, however, that the altered competitive picture cannot be so simply summarized. There does appear to be little doubt that

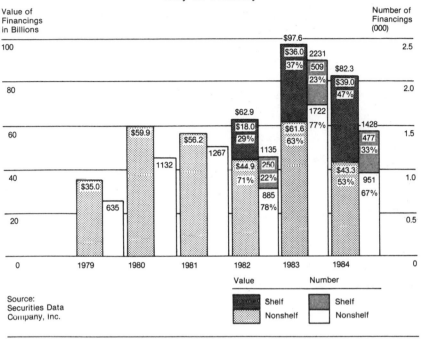

Figure 5-1
Public Financing Volume: 1979–1984
Shelf vs. Nonshelf

Source:
Securities Data
Company, Inc.

there has been vigorous competition for much of the shelf business; and this is not surprising, in view of the opportunities and benefits that would be expected to accrue to banking firms that were ultimately successful in purchasing the securities for resale. Banking firms can receive these benefits in several ways: 1) receiving direct financial contributions from the activity; 2) augmenting the supply of securities marketable through their sales networks; 3) blocking another securities firm from gaining a foothold with a traditional client; or 4) gaining the benefits of initiating a business relationship with a desirable corporate issuer.

In Figure 5-2 the data demonstrate, however, that the same group of leading underwriting originators that dominated these

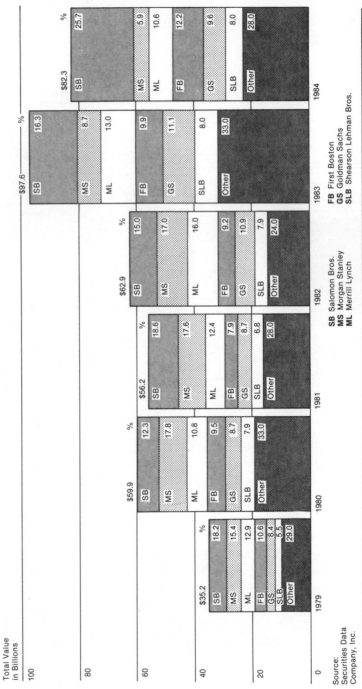

Figure 5-2
Public Financing Volume: 1979–1984
Market Shares of Top Six Firms

Total Value
in Billions

Source:
Securities Data
Company, Inc.

SB Salomon Bros.
MS Morgan Stanley
ML Merrill Lynch

FB First Boston
GS Goldman Sachs
SLB Shearson Lehman Bros.

markets before the introduction of shelf registration also has dominated them afterward. Thus, the jousting for position in the post–Rule 415 era has been confined to only a relatively small number of firms at the apex of the competitive hierarchy rather than being spread among the broader competitive group, as had been anticipated. Essentially, the leading competitor group includes the five so-called "special bracket" firms of Salomon Brothers, Morgan Stanley, Merrill Lynch, First Boston, and Goldman Sachs; Lehman (now Shearson Lehman) is often included in this top group.

These data also indicate that some important shifts have taken place in the relative standing of firms within this group of leading underwriting competitors. Figure 5-2 shows that over the entire period Salomon Brothers was the biggest gainer, with an increase in market share from 18 percent in 1979 to 26 percent in 1984. Morgan Stanley was the most prominent loser, falling from 15 percent market share in 1979 to a 7 percent share in 1984. Changes in the relative positions of other securities firms are tempered by using alternative base years and by the interpretation of the history of 1983 and 1984, since several of the underwriters suffered diminished market shares in 1984 compared to 1983.

As might have been expected, each firm's position in the shelf registration business importantly influences its overall underwriting ranking. Figure 5-3 confirms the impressive market share (37 percent) of total shelf financings taken by Salomon Brothers in 1984 compared with its 20 percent share in 1982. Equally significant is the decline in market share of shelf underwritings by Morgan Stanley, from 25 percent in 1982 to 4 percent in 1984.

While the preceding data suggest that recent realignments in competitive position have been confined to firms at the apex of the securities underwriting competitor group, there is still the question of whether the introduction of shelf underwriting has made a discernible difference in the degree of concentration within the securities-underwriting sector as a whole.

Table 5-1 shows some evidence, since 1979, of modest, increased concentration in underwriting when all securities are treated as a single group. The top fifteen investment banking firms underwrote 93 percent of all public offerings of new securi-

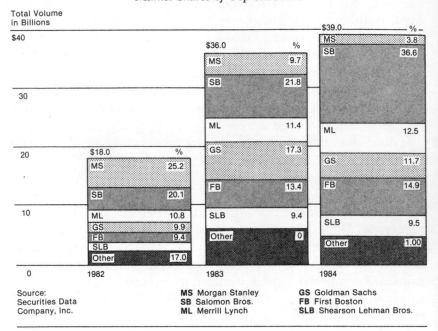

Figure 5-3
Shelf Financing: 1982–1984
Market Shares of Top Six Firms

Source:
Securities Data
Company, Inc.

MS Morgan Stanley   **GS** Goldman Sachs
SB Salomon Bros.   **FB** First Boston
ML Merrill Lynch   **SLB** Shearson Lehman Bros.

ties in 1981, the last full year before the shelf experiment. During 1982, the first year of the shelf experiment, they underwrote 95 percent; in 1983 (an aberrational year in terms of volume), 82 percent; and in 1984, under the permanent form of the rule, they underwrote 96 percent.

Overall, the basic competitive structure of the underwriting industry appears not to have been fundamentally altered by the introduction of shelf registrations. Cost savings accruing to issuers choosing the shelf route have come as a consequence of more intensive competition among a relatively few firms at the top of the underwriting hierarchy. Given the shifts in market shares among this apex group, there have been some clear gains and losses in client relationships, but again, notable shifts in market shares (with consequent gains and losses in client relationship) have been largely confined to this apex group.

Table 5-1
Dollar Volume Concentration on Selected New Issues: 1979–1984
(Individual Categories as Percentage of Overall Grand Total)[a]

		1979	1980	1981	1982	1983	1984
All Securities[b]							
Top 4	$	20.2	30.2	32.1	36.8	39.2	50.4
	%	57	50	57	59	40	61
Top 8	$	30.0	46.8	46.1	52.7	66.3	71.9
	%	85	78	82	84	68	87
Top 15	$	34.0	54.8	52.1	59.8	79.6	78.9
	%	97	92	93	95	82	96
Negotiated Debt							
Top 4	$	13.3	20.8	22.6	24.2	27.4	42.3
	%	59	57	61	59	55	65
Top 8	$	20.0	28.6	29.6	33.9	39.6	55.4
	%	88	78	80	83	80	85
Top 15	$	21.4	31.8	31.7	36.7	42.4	59.8
	%	95	87	86	90	85	92
Negotiated Equity							
Top 4	$	2.6	5.8	5.8	7.8	15.5	3.6
	%	42	38	39	43	35	28
Top 8	$	3.7	8.7	8.8	10.2	23.7	5.7
	%	60	57	60	57	53	45
Top 15	$	4.3	10.5	10.7	11.8	30.1	6.8
	%	69	68	72	66	68	54

Source: Securities Data Company, Inc.
[a] All dollar figures are in billions.
[b] "All securities" refers basically to the volume of the top fifteen firms.

CORPORATE PROFILES OF SHELF REGISTRANTS

While the introduction of the shelf registration procedure has apparently brought some significant savings to capital raisers and has had some impact on the competitive vigor within the investment banking group (albeit limited to a relatively small number at the top of the hierarchy), an equally important consideration is the impact which it is having on the "regulation by information" mandate of the Securities Act of 1933.

One outcome of the introduction of shelf registrations has been inescapable: given the usual last-minute nature of the designation of an underwriter to distribute a block of shelf registered securities, it is simply not possible for that intermediary to undertake the deliberate, independent "due diligence" investigation of the issuer's affairs contemplated by the Securities Act of 1933. Perhaps, as some argue, circumstances have changed so substantially that normal independent investigation of this kind no longer is needed. Proponents of this view presume that those corporate securities issuers utilizing the shelf option are sufficiently well known in the marketplace so that substantially all of the information considered material to the offering is already in the public domain. Further, these proponents maintain that the public securities markets are so "efficient" in absorbing this material information that the prices of securities offered in such shelf registration sales are correct and fair reflections of the attendant risks and rewards that arise owing to the nature of the companies involved.

As a means of getting a better perspective on this aspect of shelf registrations, we made an analysis of the financial and operating characteristics of the companies that actually undertook shelf filings during the first year and a half of the experimental introduction of Rule 415.[19] Prominent among these filers were firms from industry groups that are frequent capital raisers, including public utilities and financial services firms. In general, we found that most of the firms filing for *debt issues* were large corporations with assets of $1 billion or more. These issuers also tended to have a bond rating with an investment-grade designation and a fairly extensive institutional ownership. On the other hand, a considerably larger proportion of the *equity filers* were smaller in size, lacked bond ratings, and exhibited sparser institutional ownership. In sum, the debt filers, which constituted by far the largest dollar volume of shelf registrants, were by and large, substantial companies with characteristics suggesting both a certain stability in business operations and the likelihood of a broad dissemination of information about their operations. A substantial subgroup of the equity filers, however, did not fit that reassuring profile.

ADOPTION OF THE PERMANENT RULE

Following a year and a half of experience with the temporary form, the SEC revised the availability of shelf registrations and adopted Rule 415 in its permanent form. The decision was not unanimous. Adoption was passed by a vote of four to one; the chairman concurred with the majority in a separate opinion, and one commissioner concurred in the decision as it related to debt securities, but dissented as it related to equity securities. Rule 415 became effective on December 31, 1983.

Under the temporary rule, the concept of shelf registration had seemed as broad as possible; its extension to primary offerings of both debt and equity securities in effect had made the shelf technique available for most offerings of debt securities. As the Commission moved toward adoption of the permanent rule, it found that this general availability of shelf registration evoked concerns, particularly among professionals in the securities industry, about the quality and timing of adequate disclosure and the conduct of due diligence under the 1933 Securities Act.[20]

Investment bankers and broker-dealers were also concerned that the temporary rule might result in an increase in the rate of institutional dominance on the buying side of the securities markets[21] and in the further concentration of underwriting power in the securities industry; they were also concerned that it might have deleterious effects on the retail distribution of securities and on secondary securities markets. The Commission did not agree that these concerns were directly related to the issue of shelf registration. It considered Rule 415 to be a procedural rule, designed to provide an optional method of compliance with the 1933 act; it did not regard the rule as relating to any particular form or method of securities distribution.

The Commission, however, did regard questions over the adequacy of disclosure and due diligence as important issues that had a direct bearing on the statutory intent concerning the nature and quality of the information that investors should receive in a public offering of securities. It concluded that the broad availability of shelf registration, which existed under the temporary version of Rule 415, should be limited on a permanent basis to only those issuers eligible to use the short-form registration of securities under the 1933 act (Form S-3 for U.S. issuers and Form F-3 for foreign issuers). As for concerns about the nature of the diligence required to ensure appropriate disclosure, the Commission pointed to "evolving continuous due diligence by enhancing the ability of underwriters to conduct due diligence investigations of widely followed registrants."[22] In effect, the Commission felt that all important concerns regarding a permanent shelf registration rule were resolved by the existence of an efficient market engendered by the integrated disclosure system.

PROFILE OF ELIGIBILITY

In 1983 approximately 1,400 companies filed Form S-3 registration statements with the SEC. Not surprisingly, their industry classifications spanned the whole of the U.S. private sector. They were led by public utilities (8.8 percent of the group), nonelectrical machinery (7.7 percent), banking (7.5 percent), electrical products and electrical machinery (6.8 percent), chemicals and allied products (5 percent), and oil and gas companies (4.2 percent). Size of the issuers and variance in size among them was broad. Several of the more important profile characteristics of this group were particularly noteworthy:

1. Whereas they spanned a broad range; during the trial period the registrants had been predominantly large companies.
2. A substantial proportion of registrants did not possess a bond rating, and a significant proportion of those with bond ratings had a classification below the investment-grade level.
3. Institutional ownership of the groups' equity securities tended to vary directly with size, with a substantial propor-

tion of issuers in the lower-size categories having minimal institutional ownership.

4. The smaller companies in the qualifying group generally had the higher growth rates and higher price-earnings ratios; they could generally be regarded as incorporating more elements of risk than would be the case for larger firms in the qualifying group.

THE REGULATORS' POSITION

We have already pointed out that, in enacting Rule 415, the Commission took the position that the enhanced market efficiency realized under integrated disclosure would be an adequate practical surrogate for the disclosure required by the 1933 act in the case of "registrants that are widely followed in the marketplace."[23] The reasonable investigation required by the act was treated by the SEC as being subsumed in a de facto manner by integrated disclosure. In fact, the Commission explicitly stated this: "Forms S-3 and F-3 recognize the applicability of the efficient market theory to those companies which provide a steady stream of high quality corporate information to the marketplace and whose corporate information is broadly disseminated."[24]

It can be fairly argued, however, that reliance on this kind of information is not enough to fulfill the 1933 act's intent unless there is also a specific process of reasonable investigation. The available statistics suggest that the profiles of companies qualifying for shelf registration under the permanent rule are substantially more diverse than the profiles of firms that utilized Rule 415 under the temporary arrangement. This diversity encompasses comparative recent operating performance, capital structure differences, size disparities, and stock market evaluations. It seems highly unlikely that market efficiency extends without question to the bulk of this group and, therefore, it also seems unlikely that the several procedures that the SEC has identified as substitutes for normal due-diligence investigation in a shelf registration offering will suffice. The 1933 act involves, if it does not flatly require,[25] the undertaking of that specific diligence function; it establishes a disclosure requirement that is essentially the same as that provided under the 1934 act. The issuer may subjectively conclude that it is *always* diligent in determining the content of its disclosure as long as it is familiar with all data in the public domain. But this lacks the verification by an outside investigation of what may be seen as important material for the prudent investor. Indeed, as Milton Cohen commented in a 1984 review, "Disclosure for 1934 Act purposes still tends to be taken less seriously, and to be of lower quality, than those historically provided, and still aspired to, under the 1933 Act."[26]

Yet the SEC is apparently convinced that sufficient new methods of accomplishing adequate investigation have been developed in recent years, and that they have reduced to tolerable levels the potential injury from reduced or nonexistent traditional diligence that inevitably accompanies the abbreviated time schedule of a typical Rule 415 offering. It has stated that registrants—the issuers of the securities—have provided procedures for diligence investigation that have been (and are being) developed "to enable underwriters to adapt to the integrated disclosure system and the shelf registration environment." The SEC cited the registrants as the source of its information concerning "use of continuous due diligence programs, which employ a number of procedures, including designated underwriters' counsel."[27]

The SEC also has favorably noted other substitute procedures without providing any specific administrative or quasi-judicial findings as to their frequency, effectiveness, or method. It has remarked on registrants' claims that "drafting sessions" were being held in accordance with the 1934 act, in which underwriters and their counsel could participate, and that due diligence sessions were being held following the release of periodic reports.[28]

In a speech to the securities industry shortly after Rule 415 was adopted in its permanent form, SEC Chairman John Shad neither agreed with this approach nor equivocated in his remarks on these matters. He stated that "the shelf due diligence approaches suggested by non-underwriters are of limited value." Criticizing the suggestion to hold collaborative drafting sessions between issuers, groups of underwriters, and their attorneys during the preparation of prospectuses, proxies, and other SEC filing documents, he said, "Such documents are difficult enough to draft with one underwriter participating, let alone half a dozen."[29]

Shad added that continued collaboration would entail more than drafting problems: "It would be very expensive for senior corporate and underwriting executives and their attorneys to spend hundreds of thousands of hours annually, attending such meetings on the speculative possibility that the companies concerned will decide to do public offerings, and that one of the underwriters attending such sessions will be the high bidder for the issue."[30]

The Commission was aware of the problems of meeting the requirements of due diligence—whether the underwriter's investigatory function under Section 11 is considered a mandatory requirement or regarded merely as a protective shield against investor redress. The SEC has avoided this question in part by adopting Rule 176 as a statement of its views on what could be deemed compliance with the reasonable-investigation provision of Section 11 and the 1933 act. As described by the Commission, "Rule 176 sets forth a non-exclusive list of circumstances which the commission believes bear upon the reasonableness of the investigation and the determination of what constitutes reasonable grounds for belief under Section 11(b) of the Securities Act."

In applying Rule 176, the most significant problem for the investment banker's staff would be the time available for meeting the circumstances cited by the SEC. For example, how is a determination to be made as to the "availability of information with respect to the registrant"? If information is readily available and not sought, is the underwriter entitled to any shield against liability? Where pertinent information is demonstrated to be extremely difficult to acquire, is an underwriter to be excused from liability under Section 11?

In addition, the Commission seems to assume that the underwriter will be familiar with the 1934 act material incorporated by reference in the registration statement. Usually, the underwriter will *not* have participated in filing that prior report and thus will *not* have had direct knowledge of it at the time. Can the underwriter dare without more accept that the incorporated material meets the reasonable-investigation requirements of the Securities Act?

Suppose, for example, that the incorporated document is a report of an internal corporate investigation by a committee of nonmanagement directors triggered by a payment likely to be considered questionable under the Foreign Corrupt Practices

Act; or that the document is the summary of a disagreement between the Commission's chief accountant and the registrant's independent auditors as to whether a particular accounting procedure constitutes generally accepted accounting practice; or an engineering report on the causes of an accident in a foreign subsidiary of the registrant that produced a calamitous loss of life and property. In these cases, the provisions of Rule 176 may protect an underwriter for SEC purposes, but they would not serve as an impenetrable shield against the arrows of litigation in a judicial proceeding engendered by a disgruntled purchaser of an underwritten security.

CONCLUSIONS

The markets have changed dramatically in the half-century since passage of the reform legislation of the 1930s. The rise of the institutional investor and the emergence of the sophisticated, multinational corporation that is willing and able to shop widely for the best and cheapest money sources have fundamentally altered the public capital-raising process. Some of the underwriting procedures, which were originally tailored to a predominantly individual investor constituency, have clearly required modifications.

The concept of the "shelf" registration as a means of speeding up the securities-issuance process would appear to be a reasonable accommodation for well-known and frequent issuers. We have sought to demonstrate, however, that the remedy, as it was ultimately written, seriously compromises the intent of the original securities legislation whose objective is still valid in the 1980s.

Regulatory remedies in the financial services area have historically tended to appear in response to a buildup of social unhappiness with an existing set of operating conventions. One could argue that some of the remedies instituted in the 1930s were not really responsive to actual needs, but it would be hard to argue that there was no need for more and better information about securities issued in the public markets. While the markets have undoubtedly become more sophisticated and adept at ferreting out information on an informal basis, we would argue that the need for some regulation still exists for a broad group of corporate issuers. Regulators and legislators must be careful that in formulating their deregulation bath the due-diligence baby is not thrown out with the regulation water!

NOTES

1. Fifty-five percent of the growth was thus generated from 1901 to 1912, 60.0 percent from 1913 to 1922, 54.6 percent from 1923 to 1929, and virtually 100 percent from 1930 to 1939; see Raymond W. Goldsmith, *Financial Intermediaries in the American Economy Since 1900.* National Bureau of Economics Research (Princeton, N.J.: Princeton University Press, 1958).

2. Of external funds raised from 1913 to 1922, about equal proportions came from two sources: (1) public issues of debt and equity and (2) various private external debt sources, including trade credit, bank loans, mortgages, and other accruals. During the period 1923–1929, however, the amount of publicly issued debt and equity was three times as large as private external debt sources.

3. Gardiner C. Means, "The Diffusion of Stock Ownership in the United States," *Quarterly Journal of Economics* 44 (August 1930), pp. 565, 595.

4. U.S. Bureau of the Census, *Historical Statistics of the United States: Colonial Times to 1970,* series X 731-740, p. 1036.

5. Vincent P. Carosso, *Investment Banking in America* (Cambridge, Mass.: Harvard University Press, 1970), p. 68. See also Willard E. Atkins, et al., *The Regulation of the Security Markets* (Washington, D.C.: Brookings Institution, 1946), p. 27.

6. Franklin D. Roosevelt, *Public Papers* (New York: Random House, 1938), vol. I, p. 653.

7. Ibid.

8. *Economic Report of the President, 1986,* Table B-89, p. 356.

9. Department of Commerce, Bureau of the Census, *Statistical Abstract of the United States, 1985,* Table 909, p. 533.

10. Milton H. Cohen, "Truth in Securities Revisited," *Harvard Law Review* 79 (1966), p. 1340.

11. Securities and Exchange Commission, 1969, "Disclosure to Investors: A Reappraisal of Administrative Policies under the 1933 and 1934 Acts."

12. Eugene Fama, "Efficient Capital Markets: A Review of Theory and Empirical Work," *Journal of Finance* 25 (1970), p. 383.

13. Apart from failure of disclosures of material fact by issuers, acquirers, or statutory insiders whose purchases or sales may require public disclosure, however, there is always the likelihood of significant trading transactions not requiring disclosure. As long as such transactions are deemed not to be deceptive or manipulative, their impact on market prices can be known only, if at all, after they have affected market prices, possibly in a material manner. For example, the concept of arbitrage in its pure form can thrive only on riskless trading profits that derive from simultaneous price differences in two or more markets; the operation, therefore, relies on the absence of market efficiency. As trading in market index and related futures contracts—called program trading, which in itself is a market function that is not inconsistent with the concept of an efficient market—has developed, it has engendered a related, inconsistent trading impact of considerable effect (particularly on individual investors). This impact has no necessary relationship to individual securities, although it affects their prices. A typical program may involve, for example, an institu-

tion's instructions to its broker to buy or sell a list of securities of one hundred companies that are considered to represent fairly the prospects (up or down) of Standard & Poor's or any other broad index being traded by the institution through index futures contracts. The program list has analytical significance only for its function as a proxy for the index, and execution of the program may strongly influence the market prices of the securities involved, which, by hypothesis, are market leaders otherwise deemed efficiently priced. As one market observer notes, "You push a button [to put the program into effect] and, bam, it goes. There's absolutely no regard for values, just strategy." See *New York Times*, August 30, 1985, p. D1.

14. Sec. Act Rel. 5791 (December 20, 1976) [41 Fed. Reg. 56304 (1976)]; see also, Sec. Act Rel. 6235 (September 2, 1980) [45 Fed. Reg. 63693 (1980)].

15. Sec. Act Rel. 6383 (March 2, 1982) [47 Fed. Reg. 11380 (1982)] Integrated Disclosure Release. Under this framework, registrants under the 1933 act would be classified into three categories: (1) companies that are widely followed by professional analysts; (2) companies that have been subject to the periodic reporting system of the 1934 act for three or more years but are not widely followed; and (3) companies that have been in the 1934 act reporting system for less than three years. The first category would be eligible to use Form S-3, which relies upon incorporation by reference to 1934 act reports and requires minimal disclosure in the 1933 act prospectus.

16. In 1967 and 1968, concurrently with the quickening of its interest in establishing integration of disclosure provisions under the 1933 and 1934 acts, the Commission established guidelines for the initiation of a pragmatic form of shelf registration. For the nearly thirty-five years since passage of the 1933 act, the SEC had held that a conventional underwritten public offering of securities could not be registered for sale at some indefinite future time; it could not be put "on the shelf" for subsequent use. In 1968, the Commission moved to adopt what may be regarded as a conceptual forerunner of Rule 415 shelf registration. It permitted a continuous or a delayed future offering for securities to be issued in acquisition programs or securities expected to be issued on exercise of rights provided by other securities, such as conversions, options, and warrants. Sec. Act Rel. 4936 (December 9, 1968) [33 Fed. Reg. 18617 (1968)].

17. Sec. Act Rel. 6499 (November 17, 1983) [48 Fed. Reg. 52889 (1983)]. The right under the Commission's rules not to repeat information already disclosed in a public filing, but simply to refer to that filing as a source, is the basic approach to integrated disclosures under the two acts. Since the 1934 act requires periodic and extraordinary reporting, while the 1933 act reporting becomes pertinent only upon a public offering of securities, the integration is essentially a one-way street, with incorporation by reference to 1934 act public reports being used in 1933 act prospectuses without providing the information specifically.

18. David Kidwell, M. Wayne Marr, and G. Rodney Thompson, "Shelf Registration: Competition and Market Timing." Working Paper No. 192, University of Tennessee, College of Business Administration (Knoxville, July 1984); David Kidwell, M. Wayne Marr, and G. Rodney Thompson, "SEC Rule 415—The Ultimate Competitive Bid," *Journal of Financial and Quantitative Analysis* (June 1984); and Rogowski and Sorensen, "Shelf Registrations and the Cost of Capital: A Test of Market Efficiency." Working Paper. Washington State University and the University of Arizona (1983).

19. A list of all of the shelf filers during this trial period was provided by Securities Data Corporation. Financial profile characteristics were generated through the good offices of a leading New York investment banking firm.

20. At the Fifteenth Annual Institute on Securities Regulation, sponsored by the Practicing Law Institute, it was reported that Thomas A. Saunders III, of Morgan Stanley, expressed the following views on November 10, 1983, the day before the permanent Rule 415 was adopted: (1) it was not supportable that the rule would lead to lower costs for the issuer, although the issuer's administrative costs would be reduced; (2) prospectus quality had substantially decreased; (3) bid shopping, "fire drills," and a mania for "bought deals" were examples of questionable business practices that were occurring; (4) the trend toward

concentration of underwriters was accelerating; (5) issuer presentations discouraged underwriters' questions; and (6) interrogation of the biggest issuers was no longer happening, in part because of "competitive pressure" among underwriters. See *Securities Regulation and Law Report* (November 18, 1983). Special Report 15, p. 2104.

21. While not accepting the problem of institutionalization of securities markets as a pertinent consideration in its adoption of Rule 415, the Commission was clearly aware of its possible consequences to the individual investor. Speaking a year later with regard to the effect of the SEC's installation of EDGAR, its electronic data gathering system for 1934 act reports, Commissioner Charles C. Cox noted that EDGAR might reverse the trend toward institutionalization: "By revolutionizing the method by which investment decisions are made and executed, EDGAR could bring individual investors back into the stock market." *Securities Regulation and Law Report* (December 21, 1984), p. 1991.

22. Sec. Act Rel. 6499 (November 17, 1983) [48 Fed. Reg. 52889 (1983)], p. 18.

23. Ibid., p. 12.

24. Ibid.

25. Whether the investigation process is deemed mandatory, or voluntary with the underwriter who is concerned only with building a defense against possible litigation is a question that is not directly addressed in the legislative history of the 1933 act.

26. Milton H. Cohen's remarks, which were addressed to the Committee on Federal Regulation of Securities of the Section of Corporation, Banking and Business Law of the American Bar Association, were subsequently published as "The Integrated Disclosure System—Unfinished Business," 40 *The Business Lawyer* 987 (1985), p. 992.

27. Sec. Act Rel. 6499 (November 17, 1983) [48 Fed. Reg. 52889 (1983)], p. 13.

28. Ibid., p. 15.

29. See page 6 of a speech by John S. R. Shad (December 1, 1983) to the Securities Industry Association, entitled "Causes and Consequences." (See also his concurring opinion in the adoption of Rule 415, Sec. Act Rel. 6499.)

30. Ibid.

SIX

WALL STREET AND THE PUBLIC INTEREST

Warren A. Law

Nobelist James Tobin of Yale said recently, "I confess to an uneasy physiocratic suspicion, perhaps unbecoming in an academic, that we are throwing more and more of our resources, including the cream of our youth, into financial activities remote from the production of goods and services, into activities that generate high private rewards disproportionate to their social productivity."[1] The high private rewards offered by Wall Street are undeniable, but just how socially productive are its activities? The question is impossible to answer, but certainly deserves discussion.

In an ideal world skilled investment professionals will, in the words of Keynes, "defeat the dark forces of time and ignorance which envelop our future" by accurately forecasting the cash flows to be generated by an asset; and they will price the assets accordingly. Since those capital investments that are most productive will generate the largest cash flows, they will sell at the highest prices; and society's savings will be collected by investment firms and channeled thereto. In this ideal world it becomes impossible for an entrepreneur with a worthless idea—even if aided by an investment banker—to attract funds when meritorious ideas languish unfunded.

In the 1920s this fanciful image was held by many. Investment trusts appeared to provide the uninformed investor with the advantage of the experienced judgment of investment bankers. Attracted by popular articles with such titles as "Art of Investing Fast Developing Into a Science" and "Everybody Ought to be Rich," people lined up to invest. Wall Street became "the stage whereon is focused the world's most intelligent and best informed judgment of the values of the enterprises which serve men's needs."[2]

All this ended in 1929. "Rarely has a group lost so much status and respect so rapidly as had investment bankers in the three years following the great stock market crash. Their badly tarnished public image was to deteriorate still further in 1932 and 1933, as congressional committees probed deeper into their business affairs."[3] The Gray-Pecora investigation of 1932–1934, which led to the Securities Act of 1933 and the Securities Exchange Act of 1934, revealed the extent to which the real world of investment banking deviated from the ideal one represented above. Even though Pecora himself was hardly a dispassionate investigator, and in many ways his probe was mostly a spectacle, many Wall Street leaders admitted the need for substantial reform.

It is impossible to consider all of the many unpleasant practices revealed by Pecora. Some were examples of blatant fraud, and these have little relevance to my topic. But several practices *do* have continuing relevance, since to the extent they were not corrected by subsequent legislation or by changed human behavior, we may use them to provide some notion about whether— even today—Wall Street comes close to the Keynesian ideal. The following paragraphs outline some of Pecora's major targets.

SELLING PRACTICES

Numerous witnesses described the use of publicity agents to push stocks, and cash payments to newspapermen and radio announcers, who could recommend certain securities to their readers and listeners. One securities firm hired a University of Chicago professor to advertise "principles of sound investment" on a radio program; he used the radio name "Old Counsellor" and relied on scripts that were written entirely by the firm. A speaker at an Independent Bankers Association meeting, describing the pressure to sell in the 1920s, described a "continuous ringing of doorbells and telephones throughout the land."[4]

INATTENTION TO QUALITY

Pressure sales tactics are less to be deplored when the product being sold is in fact of good quality and fairly priced. With securities, regrettably, this was not always the case, particularly in respect to foreign offerings. Peruvian bonds, for example, were sold despite the fact that the underwriter's own experts had described the Peruvian government as "an adverse moral and political risk." The bonds of a Brazilian state were sold after an officer of the underwriter had written, "It would be hard to find anywhere a sadder confession of inefficiency and ineptitude than that displayed by the various state officials of Minas Gerais in respect of long-term borrowing."[5]

INADEQUATE DISCLOSURE

Today, the degree of secrecy and the obvious conflicts of interest that permeated the securities industry in the 1920s seems remarkable. Pecora found, for example, instances when reputable investment houses pushed securities on investors without revealing that the investment firm itself held extensive interests in the company whose stock was being pushed. Many investment trusts did not publish their portfolio holdings. Perhaps most surprising is how few basic facts were provided about any firm or government whose securities were being issued. It stretches our sense of credibility to learn that Singer Sewing Machine Company issued no annual reports and, as we have noted, that the president of the American Sugar Refining Company, contending that the stockholding public had no right to know the firm's profits, could state: "Let the buyer beware; that covers the whole business. You cannot wet-nurse people from the time they are born until the day they die. They have to wade in and get stuck and that is the way men are educated and cultivated."[6]

"MANUFACTURING" SECURITIES

As the appetite for securities grew during the 1920s, investment firms found it mandatory to create freshly minted securities (in today's jargon, "product") for the growing body of salesmen to peddle. Probably best known (as a result of later investigations and regulation) were the investment trusts and the public utility holding companies. Whereas only about 40 investment trusts existed before 1921, 770 had appeared by the end of 1929. Few of these provided new capital to operating companies, and in fact, most served no useful purpose other than to generate fees for the organizers. Even worse was the growing practice of using these trusts as "buyers of last resort" for slow-moving issues underwritten by the sponsors of the trusts.

Some of the need to create securities so as to "keep the pipeline full" resulted from the fierce competition for traditional issues. As Otto Kuhn of Kuhn, Loeb described it:

Fifteen American bankers sat in Belgrade, Yugoslavia, making bids, and a dozen American bankers sat in a half-dozen South and Central American states, or in Balkan States . . . one outbidding the other foolishly, recklessly, to the detriment of the public, compelling him to force bonds upon the public at a price which is not determined by the value of that security so much as by his eagerness to get it.[7]

INSIDER DEALING AND CONFLICTS OF INTEREST

Pecora uncovered innumerable instances of insider behavior that would be considered illegal today and that raised eyebrows even then. The president of Chase Bank was found, for example, to have sold his bank's stock short. Even the House of Morgan maintained a "preferred list," which included the names of many prominent political figures allowed to purchase new securities below the offering price. Again, conflicts of interest were most obvious in the investment trusts, which often lent money to, or deposited funds with, their sponsoring investment bank; even worse than this, trusts almost inevitably became the receptacles for new flotations of sponsors who euphemistically contended that this practice maintained equilibrium in the markets while a new issue was seasoning.[8]

FIFTY YEARS LATER

Unlike the Pujo investigation of 1912, which produced a long list of recommendations but resulted in no legislation, the Pecora probe yielded almost immediate results. Since the enactment of those post–Pecora laws, Wall Street has experienced almost constant scrutiny by the Securities and Exchange Commission—the agency often described as the most successful of all federal regulatory agencies—and by the private National Association of Securities Dealers (NASD), created in 1935 with the power to suspend, censure, or fine miscreants. (In 1974 alone, the NASD expelled or suspended 152 firms and 394 individuals.) With these watchdogs alive and in place then, we should be much nearer to the Keynesian ideal.

Yet George Stigler has pointed out how little we really know about the degree of success (or failure) of almost any of the governmental interventions in economic life. His study of the regulation of utility rates and its effects on American life, for example, led to a counterintuitive conclusion: "It is very doubtful whether consumers have been saved as much . . . as they have had to pay, directly and indirectly, for regulation."[9] Surely it is conceivable that regulation in the securities industry has been similarly unproductive. Yet the question has infrequently been raised, and it has rarely led to any serious investigation; perhaps this is because the answers to it are not easily quantifiable (and are thus unappealing to academics).[10] But Keynes's *General Theory of Employment, Interest and Money* itself contains almost no data since the author uses only metaphor or anecdotal evidence to support his arguments. So we may not be amiss in adopting a similar approach to the question of whether Keynes would view Wall Street more favorably in 1986 than he did a half-century ago. First, let us look again at the same issues that occupied the Pecora probe.

SELLING PRACTICES AND QUALITY

Today we still find a number of unfortunate practices: portfolio churning at the retail level; new-issue recommendations made only because their selling commissions are higher than those of others; and the investing of widows' funds in options and other imprudent gambles. But there is reason to believe that the problem of selling practices, at least in larger firms, is less serious than it once was. This improvement does not necessarily demonstrate any improvement in the standards of the average account executive; rather, it documents the effectiveness of the compliance officers who now operate at every large firm and are supported with massive computer programs designed to detect aberrant sales behavior. Today the risks to a firm's reputation are too great for violations by any single broker to be tolerated, especially since the SEC also uses its own comprehensive, computerized surveillance programs, and it is widely believed that "the SEC tries its cases in the newspapers."[11]

On the other hand, any advocate of truth-in-advertising

might question the typical wire-house advertising, which implies the immediate, supervisory presence of a highly trained account executive who is knowledgeable about every facet of investments, potential changes in legislation, etc.—a sort of financial counselor with only the customer's welfare in mind. That image is difficult to reconcile with the comment made by a director of a wire-house training program:

> If you go before a bunch of registered reps who haven't established a business yet, forget about honesty. They're going to say anything to make a sale. For most of them, the classes we give in compliance are like a criminal learning what the law is—he wants to know how far he can go without its being a felony. . . . You give them six months training, then put them in a situation where all the pressure is to make sales. When the market goes bad, they get panicky, even those whose personalities would incline them to comply. I don't blame them.[12]

Only an innocent could fail to recognize some truth in this description. The fact remains that it can be argued that securities are as much *sold* as they are bought, and newly underwritten issues involving "assignment of local sales quotas, mandatory evening and weekend solicitation sessions, and extra inducements to salesmen" (an SEC description of one firm's sales technique) not only do not fit the image projected in television advertisements, but also sound suspiciously like the "ringing of doorbells and telephones throughout the land" of the 1920s. Thus, we are not surprised when one study finds that investors who bought shares in initial public offerings of industrial equities during 1949–1963 did not earn as much as they would have if they had invested in the market as a whole, despite the higher risk of these unseasoned issues.[13] In short, it seems possible the new issues were oversold (see Table 6-1).

Similarly, Professor Stigler conducted his own simple test in 1963: he hypothetically bought every substantial new issue of industrial common stocks from 1923 to 1928 and from 1948 to 1955; next, he calculated the value of both portfolios after a five-year holding period. He found no important difference between the pre–SEC and post–SEC portfolios.[14] Although his experiment has been justifiably criticized on grounds of statisti-

Table 6-1
Long-Run Annual Rate of Return

Investment	Return	
	1949–1963	1953–1963
Original Industrial Issues	16.5%	9.0%
Standard & Poor Industrials	18.7%	17.0%

Source: See note 13.

cal oversimplicity, nevertheless it leaves some observers with a sense of disquiet that is reinforced by an SEC study of over 500 initial public offerings issued during the seven-year period that ended in 1962.[15] This 1967 SEC study found that 42 percent of the firms were bankrupt, 12 percent had disappeared, and 20 percent were losing money.

Unfortunately these studies are now decades old, and later studies do not cover a holding period long enough to ensure valid results. There seems to be no way to measure scientifically the *average* quality of the new securities being offered today and then compare them to the performance of securities in the 1920s. But we may introduce anecdotal evidence.

In 1929 National City Company accumulated a block of Anaconda Copper Mining stock, recommended it to its customers as "a sound investment" (at more than $100 per share), and then watched it fall to $4 per share by 1932. Similarly, in the first two months of 1986, 94 "blind pools" were filed with the SEC for registration; in many of these pools, the investor will be fortunate to lose only 96 percent of his investment. Of course, it can be argued that while National City was a leading financial institution, most blind pools today are underwritten by small firms, many of which will eventually join the ranks of NASD expellees. But some feeling of unease remains.

One obvious change since the 1920s is the domination of markets by institutional investors who, presumably, are competent to judge quality and who are immune to salesmen's blandishments. At the same time, however, investment firms that do a retail brokerage business alongside institutional block trading face obvious conflicts of interest that did not exist in the 1920s. Long ago, the SEC expressed its concern that such firms might seek to avoid the risk of positioning a block of securities by placing it in discretionary retail accounts; in fact, the SEC described several instances where this had happened.[16] The problem created here may appear to need no comment, but the issue is more subtle: even if the block is *not* placed in discretionary accounts, "securities are made available at retail in connection with a block transaction only when wholesale customers cannot be found, and presumably the wholesale customers know what they are doing."[17] Some firms rationalize this conflict by making certain that their research department independently recommends the stock. The reader will have to decide whether this is sufficient protection against abuse.

INADEQUATE DISCLOSURE

If anything on Wall Street has changed since the 1920s, it is the amount of information available to an investor. Although the Investment Bankers Association (and others) had long pressed for greater disclosure, it was not achieved until the Securities Act of 1933 made the now familiar issuing company's prospectus a lawful requirement, along with regulatory verification of its completeness. Moreover, the act made the investment banker liable for the exercise of what has come to be called "due diligence" in examining the issuer's affairs and describing them adequately in the prospectus. Under the due diligence doctrine, the banker is legally required to exercise the care "required of a prudent man in the management of his own property." Yet it is generally conceded that the typical prospectus provides little help to the individual investor; some question whether investors read them at all. Indeed, a really "full" disclosure could overwhelm a reader and submerge the truly important facts in minutiae. We have all seen prospectuses that fit Judge Weinstein's description: ". . . a literary art form calculated to communicate as little of the essential information as possible while exuding an air of total candor."[18]

The president of American Sugar may have been right: investors have to "wade in and get stuck" to learn their lesson. Certainly the warning on each prospectus—"These Securities Should Not Be Purchased By Investors Who Cannot Assume A Total Loss On Their Investments"—ordinarily serves merely to whet the investor's appetite. When Digital Switch Corporation

had a successful 1980 offering at $5 per share, the prospectus
pointed out that three outside firms had each estimated that the
fair market value did not exceed $.01 per share; and several
pages discussed "Special Risk Factors," among them the fact that
accountants could not determine how much stock was already
outstanding.

If our present full disclosure remains inadequate to protect the
public, we may still fall back on the reputation of the underwriting investment firm, as in pre–1933 days. This protection as-
sumes, however, that due diligence has, in fact, been exercised.
Since the *BarChris* decision of 1968, investment bankers have
been more careful in this regard, although they have made occa-
sional missteps as well. In 1982, however, the introduction of
Rule 415 changed the game; with shelf registration, due diligence obviously becomes impossible, and investment bankers
simply arrange a "bought deal." The Securities Industry Association almost immediately asked the SEC to repeal the rule, cit-
ing, among other things, the need for greater time in which
underwriters could investigate issues. John Whitehead, possibly
the most vocal opponent of the rule, has contended that the
limited disclosure involved in shelf registration "threatens to
sweep away 50 years of investor protection and return the new-
issue market to the jungle environment of the 1920's."[19]

Supporters of the rule, which has subsequently been limited to
issuers with over $150 million of stock held by outside investors,
contend that firms of this size are well known and do not require
much investigation. Moreover, they argue that most securities
sold off the shelf are sold to institutional investors, who presumably are competent to judge an issue without a forty-page prospectus, and that much larger, secondary trading markets operate satisfactorily without due diligence. After more than four
years' experience, it now seems unlikely that the rule will be
revoked, since (to date) no debacle has occurred to support John
Whitehead's gloomy prediction. Nevertheless, there may be relevance in his concern. In today's volatile environment, the
condition of even a large firm can change with surprising sud-
denness. Moreover, it has been shown that, although the SEC
apparently believed it was reducing the universe of permissible
issuers under Rule 415 when it issued its permanent rule in 1984,
the universe of qualifiers under the "stronger" rule is even more

diverse than it had been under the temporary rule; it now includes subsets of firms with characteristics that suggest the possibility of fairly rapid obsolescence of information.[20]

The investment banking firm Salomon Brothers has had ex-
ceptional success under this rule; one investment banker has
even said, "It was almost written for Salomon Brothers." Thus it
is surprising to find John Gutfreund, president of Salomon
Brothers, echoing John Whitehead in remarks that he made on
Rule 415 in 1982:

> [Rule 415] allows a process to occur that was formerly
> anathema. The underwriting process now overwhelmingly
> favors the issuer over the investor, [allowing] issuers access
> to any market with extreme rapidity and with almost any
> kind of vehicle which cannot be properly scrutinized by
> other bankers or potential investors. . . . [Thus] we are
> going to be the subject in a few years time to what I call
> reregulation. That will only come after some major disloca-
> tions, which I think we will probably see fairly soon.[21]

Not many years ago, a firm's ties with its traditional investment banker could have been described as nearly connubial.
Since Rule 415, as one investment banker puts it, we have
moved "from the traditional concept of marriage to one-night
stands." In contrast, the Securities Act of 1933 has been described as "the quintessential sunshine law." When Franklin
Roosevelt sent it to Congress, he said, "This proposal adds to
the ancient rule of *caveat emptor*, the further doctrine 'let the
seller also beware.' It puts the burden of telling the whole truth
on the seller."[22] What is not clear under Rule 415 is how much
of the burden of uncovering the whole truth the investment
banker can assume in an offering that he buys and resells within
fifteen minutes. As one observer has said: "The true test of the
shelf rule will come in the next bear market."

While the adequacy of mandated corporate disclosure is debatable, the costs are not. Over 50,000 documents are filed
annually with the SEC, and one study estimated that in 1975
corporations had filing costs of $213 million for such periodic
forms as 10-K and 10-Q and $193 million for new-issue disclo-
sures.[23] Adjusting for inflation and for documents excluded by
the study, the costs today probably approximate $1 billion per
year, despite Rule 415.

In view of these costs, the conclusions of George J. Benston are interesting. He studied shareholder returns in 466 NYSE companies for the periods before and after the SEC was established. Of these companies, 296 already had voluntarily disclosed information in the pre–SEC era. Not only did Benston's results confirm the random walk hypothesis, pre– and post–SEC, but the similarity between the disclosure and nondisclosure groups led him to conclude that disclosure requirements "had no measurable positive effect on the securities traded on the NYSE."[24]

INSIDER DEALING

In recent years, the SEC has assigned an extremely high priority to preventing trading on the basis of insider information, and it has monitored the markets with the help of sophisticated computer programs. But at the same time, the financial rewards from such insider trading have increased with the risk of exposure. The growth of hostile tender offers, coupled with the increased availability of options on stocks and the use of foreign accounts to trade on American markets, has created opportunities for quick and substantial profits from inside information on a scale not seen heretofore. Since 1980, the first year a criminal case was filed, there have been forty-one convictions for insider trading.[25]

Most of the publicized cases have involved some aspect of mergers or acquisitions. In 1978, Morgan Stanley was accused of revealing confidential earnings projections of Olinkraft (information that it had obtained from discussions with another client about a merger) to help Johns-Manville win a bidding war for Olinkraft. This incident attracted unusual attention because of Morgan Stanley's reputation for utter probity in all its activities, and the firm placed an advertisement in The Wall Street Journal to defend itself. The advertisement commented on the activities of Morgan Stanley's arbitrage department in dealing in Olinkraft shares; it pointed out that the firm followed "the well-known industry practice of maintaining a 'Chinese Wall' between the merger and acquisition and arbitrage departments."

Risk arbitrageurs (arbs) are, in fact, almost universally believed by outsiders to rely heavily on inside information (obtained from within the arbitrageur's own firm or otherwise).

Arbs naturally deny that they use such information, but one prominent arbitrageur has remarked, "We don't write any memos." A CEO of a major brokerage house has said about insider trading, "If you really want to stop a lot of the trading, the SEC should forbid investment houses from engaging in arbitrage activity. No matter what they tell you about Chinese Walls, they're more like curtains."[26] In fact, the arrest of Dennis B. Levine and the plea bargaining of Ivan Boesky on charges of massive insider trading may support this conclusion, and the press predicted that plea bargaining would lead to a "Wall Street version of Watergate" and "expose the existence of a vast information-trading ring."[27]

MANUFACTURING SECURITIES

The high fixed costs of brokerage houses, the end of fixed commissions, and the diminishing spreads on traditional underwritings have inevitably led firms to create a steady stream of new products to fill the brokerage pipeline and maintain margins. The public utility holding companies of the 1920s have been replaced with real estate syndications, drilling programs, commodity straddles, and variable annuities. Some firms have expressed the goal of becoming a "financial supermarket"—an unfortunate choice of words since, in the 1920s, National City Corporation chose to describe itself as a "financial department store" and the Pecora investigation uncovered the ultimate, seamy results of that corporation's business.

Undoubtedly the most fertile field recently opened for new "securities" has been that of options and futures contracts. Yet these do not represent an unalloyed benefit to the economic system, as Professor Tobin has noted:

Collectively they contain considerable redundancy. Every financial market absorbs private resources to operate, and government resources to police. The country cannot afford all the markets that enthusiasts may dream up. In deciding whether to approve contracts for trading, the authorities should consider whether they really fill gaps in the menu . . . not just opportunities for speculation and financial arbitrage.[28]

CONFLICTS OF INTEREST

Conflict of interest is inescapable in investment banks; it arises largely from the multiple roles played by the investment banker. In the typical underwriting, for example, the banker stands between the issuer, who wants the best price for the security, and the buyer, who desires the lowest price. If the investment banker later makes a secondary market in the security, more conflicts may be introduced. The biblical observation that no man can serve two masters, if strictly followed, would make many of Wall Street's present activities impossible.[29] Yet there clearly are efficiencies to be gained by allowing the investment banker to wear two (or several) hats, and Wall Street is not unique, of course, in this regard. Commercial banks underwrite municipal bonds, make markets in them, and manage clients' bond portfolios; and it was once common practice for banks to use the commissions generated by their trust departments to attract deposits from brokers.

Nevertheless, one may still question whether some easily avoidable conflicts offer much potential for abuse. In 1985, for example, one prominent new venture-oriented U.S. investment bank won a proxy battle to manage a British investment trust; the U.S. bank intended to liquidate the trust's assets and reinvest them in companies in which the bank had already invested and planned eventually to take public. This arrangement was strongly reminiscent of the situation in the 1920s.[30]

Similarly, of the potentials for conflict in management buyouts (MBO's), which almost always involve an investment banker, one seems most clear: management, which owes a fiduciary duty to outside stockholders, is negotiating to purchase the firm from those same stockholders. As Professor Lowenstein of Columbia Law School puts it, "No change in social acceptance can mask . . . the potentially raw breach of loyalty when the management of a corporation undertakes to buy the business from its owners at a time, and where possible at a price, of its own choosing."[31] This conflict becomes more severe for the investment banker when, as is increasingly the case, the banker not only structures the deal but is also an investor in it. In addition, the banker may expect continuing fees for advising the company and thus is even more concerned than usual that the deal be consummated.

Once management has decided to sell the company, the conflict inherent in an MBO may be so great that there should be a rule mandating an open auction. Even then, some conflicts would remain, since management and the investment banker have such obvious advantages as insider information and the probable support of the board of directors. Rather than promote open bidding, however, there is a tendency for management (and their investment-banker advisers) to try to preempt the bidding. Since an MBO usually takes several months to arrange, we have seen the rise of the "tender buyout"; in this two-step approach, management and the investment banker first tender for a firm's shares, and once in control, they refinance through traditional leveraged-buyout techniques. Completing the deal in twenty business days (which the Williams Act requires for a tender offer) rather than in several months reduces the chance of losing the deal to a higher bidder.

Another preemptive approach was used in the attempted Northwest Energy MBO, where the directors granted an investment banker (who was to participate as an investor in the MBO) an option to purchase the company's most valuable asset, a pipeline, in an attempt to defeat a bid, which was 29 percent higher, from another firm. Eventually, the investment banker received $26 million from the acquirer for cancelling this option—money that might otherwise have gone to stockholders.[32]

A TENTATIVE BALANCE SHEET

From all this fragmentary evidence we might conclude that, after fifty years, Keynes would have no difficulty recognizing Wall Street. This conclusion might have been anticipated, since history suggests that regulatory constraints in financial institutions usually lead to unintended results.[33] And, above all, neither human nature nor the type of individual attracted to work on the Street is likely to have changed in the intervening half-century. One of the inevitable, and regrettable, results of the remarkably high incomes common in the securities industry is that a few of those in the industry seem motivated almost solely by money, and these few are willing to cut corners to get it. Thus we have seen instances of individuals who already earn million-dollar incomes acting in clearly illegal ways in order to earn even more. The same motive seems largely to account for the growing numbers of Wall Streeters who jump from firm to firm.[34]

But even if Wall Street were populated entirely by seminarians, it does not follow that the Street would act to promote Keynes's ideal social purpose and "direct new investment into the most profitable channels in terms of future yield," since as he suspected, "the best brains of Wall Street have been, in fact, directed towards a different object."[35]

Keynes's argument was that Wall Street in his time was dominated not by true investors but by speculators who were "concerned, not with what an investment is really worth . . . but with what the market will value it at, under the influence of mass psychology, three months or a year hence." Oddly, he thought this result inevitable, for as the market's liquidity improved, it became easier to speculate. Keynes reminds us that we may pay a penalty in instability for the greater liquidity of our markets: "It is as though a farmer, having tapped his barometer after breakfast, could decide to remove his capital from the farming business between 10 and 11 in the morning and reconsider whether he should return to it later in the week."

Assuming it was accurate in 1936, does Keynes's analysis fit in 1986? In view of all the strides made in recent years in modern portfolio and asset pricing theory (from the Capital Asset Pricing Model to Arbitrage Pricing Theory, and beyond) and the rise of institutional investors who use these theories (and employ academic theorists to develop others), is it not probable that the markets today are dominated by investors who, unperturbed by the gunslingers, ignore near-term market fluctuations and seek the true, intrinsic, long-term value of a stock?

Apparently many financial theorists, and perhaps a majority, think so; they subscribe to the "efficient markets hypothesis" (EMH)—the belief that stock market prices actually reflect underlying values and that, contrary to Keynesian theory, changes in prices reflect changes in intrinsic values and not changes in the possibly irrational opinions of traders. EMH has been described as "the best established fact in all of the social sciences." Yet some theoreticians disagree. In his 1985 presidential address to the American Finance Association, Fischer Black argued that share prices might diverge from value by substantial amounts for prolonged periods of time; and Professor Shiller of Yale has shown that markets fluctuate much more than can be explained by changes in rationally formed expectations.[36]

I suspect that most of Wall Street disagrees, as I do, with the EMH; after all, in its strongest form, it argues the near uselessness of the vast research effort devoted to finding "undervalued situations." And any sentient observer of the rise and fall of shares in computer-leasing companies, mobile-home manufacturers, REIT's, and other industries (the list is almost endless) should be skeptical of the EMH, at least in its strong form. Anyone who watched a stock as thoroughly studied as IBM move from 55 to 134 to 99 to 128 in a recent thirty-month period might well subscribe instead to the Keynesian view of the market.

Two recent factors make it even more likely that Keynes's description still applies. One is the rise of "program trading"— the related buying and selling of stocks and stock index futures—which apparently breeds volatility in the market.[37] An episode in March 1986, when 57 million shares changed hands on the New York Stock Exchange in the final half-hour, resulting in the fourth-largest decline in the Dow Jones index in history, exemplifies the problem. Although it has been estimated that fewer than one hundred traders play this game, such trading may account for 25 percent of NYSE volume. Certainly it is difficult to believe that these "investors" are attempting to judge the intrinsic long-run value of the companies whose securities they buy and sell at the suggestion of a computer.

A second new element is the rise of the unfriendly takeover. Again, it is equally difficult to envision arbitrageurs being concerned with the long-term value of stocks they are accumulating. Instead, they have only one interest: "Will the deal go through?" One leading arb admits that he is not normally buying or selling securities because of their investment value: "If you're caught when a merger falls through, then you become . . . an investor."[38]

When we consider the proper allocation of our national capital resources, the mispricing that results from short-run market myopia becomes most important when a stock offering is involved. The ability to issue stock at an unusually favorable price has the same effect on a firm as the ability to borrow at an unusually low rate of interest. If the stock price does not represent intrinsic value, then capital markets are inefficient (i.e., valuations do not accurately reflect the future payments associated with the security), and some firms may have access to funds when equally deserving ones do not.

If the stock offering is an initial public offering (IPO), another sort of mispricing may demonstrate market irrationality, or investment banker inadequacy, or both. As already noted, the investment banker must reconcile the interests of both issuer and buyer when setting the terms of an IPO. In general, bankers rationalize their position by "letting the market set the price" (i.e., comparing the new issue with similar issues already trading and pricing it accordingly). Indeed, one characteristic of a good investment banker is a "feel for the market," which refers to the ability to understand how a security will trade after issuance. One of the selling points of those firms that maintain heavy trading activities is the argument that only in this way can a firm develop this understanding, particularly in today's volatile market environment. Rule 415 has strengthened this argument.

Mispricing an IPO is almost immediately obvious; it is usually an embarrassment (if the issue quickly rises to a premium) or a source of pain (if it must be marked down in order to get rid of it) to the banker. But there are exceptions, especially with an initial equity offering that the public expects to be "hot." Some investment bankers contend that, in this case, they still try to price at "fair" value no matter what the investor is willing to pay. This may explain the pricing of Morgan Stanley Group's initial public offering, which was offered at $56.50 per share; it jumped immediately to $70 and climbed to $74.25 on the first day.

It is difficult to believe that so wide a divergence can be adequately explained by the lack of "market feel" alone. Reportedly, the initial price was set by Morgan's comanagers so as to avoid conflicts of interest. The fact that the original estimated offering price was $42 to $46 a share indicates how difficult the pricing process is, particularly when we note that (a) Morgan is not an early-stage, high-technology firm (indeed, it has a well-documented earnings history) and (b) equities of similar firms, like First Boston, were already trading.

In sum, then, Wall Street may be better at allocating the

nation's savings today than a half-century ago, but it still doesn't
do a very good job. This failure has enabled followers of Benjamin Graham and other contrarians to generate superior investment results; the fact that so few investors have followed this
approach suggests that misallocation of resources is less the fault
of the Street than of human nature. Keynes was a shrewd observer; he recognized that the inevitable result of human predis-
position was a market that resembled a casino and that "when
the capital development of a country becomes a byproduct of a
casino, the job is likely to be ill done."

Perhaps, then, we are fortunate that so little of the real investment by nonfinancial corporations depends on raising new
external funds. As Table 6-2 shows, in the latest recession,
internal funds (after dividends) exceeded capital expenditures.

Moreover, mispricing may be more serious in equity than in
debt instruments, and stock offerings usually total only a small
fraction of debt offerings. So we should not overstate the case
against Wall Street as an allocator of capital, particularly when a
few academics argue that insider trading promotes rather than
harms efficiency.[39]

THE MERGERS AND ACQUISITIONS
PHENOMENON

On the other hand, one phenomenon almost unknown to
Keynes is now such a big business that it dominates much of the

Table 6-2
Sources of Funds and Capital Expenditures of
Nonfarm Nonfinancial Corporations ($ billions)

	Sources			Capital Expenditures
	Total	Internal	Securities and Mortgages	
1975	157.0	119.7	20.9	109.7
1980	335.2	189.5	52.4	221.2
1982	309.4	234.3	43.9	229.6
1984	487.4	334.8	(15.9)	367.8

Source: *Economic Report of the President 1986*, Table B-89.

thinking of investment bankers and investors: mergers and acquisitions (M&A). It is only a slight exaggeration to say that the
phenomenon could not exist without the aid (connivance, some
would say) of Wall Street, and no discussion of the Street (or in
the Street) is complete without some attention to M&A; this is
especially true of unfriendly takeovers. Table 6-3 shows the recent growth of M&A activity.

Those academics who support the EMH most strongly also
argue heatedly that takeovers are socially desirable, since they
"improve efficiency, transfer scarce resources to higher valued
uses, and stimulate effective corporate management" (the words
of the 1985 *Economic Report of the President*).[40] Their support is
not surprising; the share price of target firms usually increases
materially after a takeover bid, and because EMH believers hold
that share prices accurately reflect intrinsic value, they assert
that something must have happened as a result of the takeover
to increase the true value of the target company (and thus create
additional wealth, Q.E.D.).[41]

Since I have already explained my distrust of the EMH, it is
understandable that I also hold antithetical views to those expressed by people who extoll the benefits of takeovers.[42] I suspect that the ultimate outcome of the recent takeover binge will
be economically damaging and that Wall Street must bear some
responsibility. At the same time, it is difficult to contend that,
when they help a client consummate or foil a raid, investment
bankers should be concerned with social welfare. Surely while
the social issues remain debatable and when fees are so large, we
cannot expect bankers to adopt the role of business-statesmen.

Table 6-3
Net Merger-Acquisition Announcements

	Number	Value ($ billions)	Deals Over $100 Million
1980	1,889	44.3	94
1981	2,395	82.6	113
1982	2,346	53.8	116
1983	2,533	73.1	138
1984	2,543	122.2	200
1985	3,001	179.8	270

Source: *Mergerstat Review 1985*. (Chicago: W. T. Grimm and Co., 1986), pp. 3, 9.

Nevertheless, M&A seems to bring out the dark side of investment banking, not only with regard to insider trading, but in
other respects as well.

The fees for investment banks, for example, in some widely
publicized deals have been staggering in both absolute terms and
in relation to the working time involved. (Since the investment
banker rarely has any capital at risk, it may be argued that as
with a lawyer's fee, M&A fees represent a reward only for time
spent.) Morgan Stanley, for example, reportedly received as
much as $30 million in Pantry Pride's takeover of Revlon, and
Lazard Frères and Co. got $11 million. First Boston received
$126,582 per hour of work on the Texaco-Getty takeover. It
does not require utter cynicism to suggest that potential rewards
as big as these may well distort an investment banker's judgment, even without the banker being conscious of any such
influence. The human capacity for rationalization is almost lim-
itless.

FAIRNESS OPINIONS

As a further example of ambiguous areas, consider the ubiqui-
tous "fairness opinion." Recent legal decisions have shown the
degree to which directors may be unwise if they make or accept a
takeover offer without first receiving a brief letter from an investment banker opining that the offer is fair and equitable to
the shareholders (the phrase "from a financial point of view"—
whatever that may imply—is usually added). The fee for such a
letter is likely to be several hundred thousand dollars, and the
letter may also involve a bonus if the deal is finally consummated.

Since I have argued that security evaluation is at best an
arcane art, there is obviously room here for differences of opinion (as in the Morgan Stanley pricing example). Dean Burton
G. Malkiel of Yale has contended: "There is, I believe, a fundamental indeterminateness about the value of common shares
even in principle. God Almighty does not know the proper
price-earnings multiple for a common stock."[43] Thus, it is not
surprising to find conflicting fairness opinions offered by reputable investment banks.

Occasionally eyebrows are raised, however. In 1980, for instance, Cavenham Holdings, Inc. asked Diamond International shareholders to vote against Diamond's planned acquisition of Brooks-Scanlon, Inc. A prominent investment bank wrote a fairness opinion backing the Brooks-Scanlon acquisition, despite the fact that the same investment firm had previously represented Cavenham in two earlier deals and had reportedly demanded a $3 million fee to represent them in this one. After Cavenham rejected that amount as "excessive," one investment banker theorized that the fairness opinion was written "to get even with Jimmy Goldsmith for not hiring them in this deal."[44] Cavenham then turned to another investment firm, which wrote an "unfairness" opinion for $200,000.

No reputable firm would write an opinion without some study of comparable deals, and it must be willing to testify as to the basis for its opinion in any subsequent litigation. I do not contend that investment bankers are in effect saying, "What answer do you want?"; but I do note that, when reasonable men differ, it takes superhuman character to ignore the very large fee forthcoming for the "right" answer.

CONTINGENCY FEES

In most M&A transactions, the investment banker's fee is contingent on the outcome of the deal. Indeed, a recent study of tender offers from January 1978 to February 1983 found that only 12 percent of target firms and 7 percent of bidders paid fees independent of the outcome of the offer. The difference in fees between "successful" and "unsuccessful" deals is not trivial.

Several investment bankers have expressed concern that disparities of this size make it very difficult for an investment banker to render dispassionate advice; instead, a "win at any price" attitude prevails.

If the client wants to win a targeted acquisition, why should an investment banker force its reservations about the move on an unwilling client? The investment banker advising Sohio in its disastrous acquisition of Kennecott Copper recalls, ". . . our assignment was clearly not to give them our views on the future likelihood of copper prices. . . . Our views were solicited on how to execute the deal."[45] In defense of this situation, another banker has said, "The long-term reputational interest of the

firm, in terms of repeat business, is a sufficient guarantee against
the moral hazard problem of recommending terrible deals in
order to get fees."[46] At the same time, however, the CEO of yet
another investment firm states:

> The investment banker has got to have some conscience
> about what he is doing. . . . As you move to a transactional
> world there's no incentive for him to have a conscience. In
> fact, there's almost a disincentive for him to advise a corpo-
> ration on what he really thinks the corporation ought to do;
> rather he is more oriented towards how he is going to earn a
> fee out of this.[47]

All of these comments probably contain some truth. But it is
disquieting to read a description of an investment banker who
"makes no bones about his desire to prove that he can pull off a
major takeover as successfully as . . . First Boston."[48] It is even
worse to read that another one told executives of Beatrice, "I put
you in play. But it's not too late"—suggesting the bank might
help fend off a takeover.[49] One firm has been accused of putting
its own client in play, and another is allegedly grooming its own
corporate raider. Some critics contend that investment bankers
are now the main factor motivating hostile takeovers, and surely
high fees have exerted some influence.[50]

TACTICS

It is exceedingly difficult to know where the foul lines should
be drawn for the game that is euphemistically called "the contest
for corporate control," especially when important macho in-
stincts become aroused. Lawyers have experienced the same
problem; despite a highly detailed code of professional responsibility, they often display the attitude that almost anything goes
in legal combat, since judge and jury will decide the winner.
Investment bankers have much less rigidly codified rules of behavior, so perhaps they should not be disparaged for occasionally
transgressing the blurred line between the short-run interests of
the client and the banker's own responsibility as a citizen. Here,
the unanswerable question concerns the extent to which the
banker is a mere technician who is hired to do a job: are bankers
free of responsibility for what happens after they deliver the
goods, or do they have a duty to press clients to think beyond

their own legal responsibilities to broader issues of public policy? Clearly, investment bankers have an obligation not to partici- pate in any deal that oversteps the parameters of the law. But do they also have an obligation to press their client by arguing (in a less obvious situation), "This is just not the right thing for a decent firm to do"?

For example, in the famous "midnight special" deal, when the Sun Company attempted an overnight capture of Becton Dick- inson while the markets were closed, those involved were sufficiently aware of the nature of their actions to have the temerity to entitle the proposed new firm (to be used as an acquisition vehicle) "L.H.I.W., Inc."; later, the title was re- vealed under oath to be an acronym for "Let's Hope It Works." At least one investment banker also carefully arranged for indemnification by Sun in case the deal ran into legal difficulty (a wise precaution, as it turned out). Meanwhile, another in- vestment firm, which managed a mutual fund holding a large block of Becton Dickinson stock, tendered the stock and col- lected an investment banking fee from Sun on the side.

Even while hesitating to join the ranks of knee-jerk business critics who condemn so many actions in the takeover arena, it is possible to argue that some business managers and their bankers, by playing fast and loose, are actually inviting the increased regulation that their foes have been demanding. As two thoughtful observers have agreed:

> When one sees two great corporations forcing each other, without shareowner reference, into positions of equal impo- tence, it is natural to ask how such an event is consistent with public trust and confidence, which all recognize as indispensable to the continuance of the corporate system. If the legitimacy of corporate management becomes uncertain in the public mind, sweeping legislation may be expected. The great affairs that are left to corporate governance are too near the heart of our economy to remain unnoticed.[51]

CONCLUSION

At the start, I asked whether Keynes would give a better grade to Wall Street in 1986 than he did in 1936. The answer is unclear. We still see an unfortunately large share of the nation's scarce savings frittered away in misguided investments; the use of inside information is widespread; and Wall Street's role in our present takeover binge—a consideration which did not exist in 1936—is worrisome when one believes, as I do, that takeovers do not lead to the best of all possible worlds. Finally, the trend toward "financial department stores" seems likely to produce even greater conflicts of interest than we have already seen.

Can the situation be improved by even more regulation? Certainly, there is no shortage of suggestions: it has been proposed, for example, that we reduce conflicts of interest by splitting the broker-dealer function or by divorcing investment banking from market making; others suggest that state blue-sky laws should be replaced by federal regulation of the fairness and validity of an offering; and several bills have been introduced in Congress to regulate takeovers. With respect to these proposals, it seems better to bear the ills we have than to flee to others we know not of; the mind reels, for example, at the thought of government bureaucrats evaluating the merits of new issues. And any breakup of investment firms would reduce economies of scale, deprive various functions of needed capital, and weaken the flexibility and speed of response that is the pride of American capital markets; and this is particularly unwise as we move toward an integrated global money market.

Perhaps our best hope is to reemphasize the sense of personal and institutional responsibility that each investment banker should have. While there is no credible evidence that individual bankers are today less (or more) responsible or ethical, three important changes have undeniably occurred. First, as Table 6-4 shows, investment firms are now much bigger. Morgan Stanley, which had a corporate finance staff of 33 in 1965, today has 200 in M&A alone. Any problem, such as the building of a Chinese Wall between investment banking functions, increases in difficulty and scope almost geometrically with firm size.

Similarly, some uninformed people have found it difficult to believe that E. F. Hutton's top officers remained unaware of their firm's cash management practices that attracted so much unfavorable publicity in 1985. But experienced managers understand how difficult it is to know what 17,000 people are doing at more than 400 different locations. Indeed, Theodore Morgan argues persuasively that, given the fundamental nature of large

Table 6-4
New York Stock Exchange Membership

	Number of Firms	Offices	Registered Personnel	Estimated Pre-Tax Profit ($ Millions)
1950	620	1,661	11,409	NA
1975	494	3,425	35,682	415
1980	570	4,421	48,435	1,158
1985	599	6,144	75,011	2,112

Source: NYSE, *Fact Book 1986*, pp. 82, 83.

institutions, a leader is almost inevitably divorced from much of reality.[52]

In view of these difficulties, it is disturbing to read of cases where even rudimentary attempts at reducing abuse were overlooked. In 1979, for example, a reporter noted: "In at least two major investment banking houses . . . low-level employees are still not being told, even at orientation time, that confidential information must be kept secret and may not be traded on."[53]

A second important change is that we have entered the era of "transactional finance" and left behind, probably forever, the days of long-term "relationships" between banker and client. The increased sophistication and internationalization of modern capital markets probably make this shift inevitable. But part of the price we pay is a weakening of the *sense of consequence*—the realization that present actions will have consequences for both banks and clients years into the future—among investment bankers. The CEO of one investment firm recently made this point, plaintively and perhaps with some hyperbole: "Nobody in our business is responsible or accountable for what they do. If a deal closed yesterday, forget it, you're on to the next. If it doesn't work out a year from now, who cares? That bothers me."[54]

The third change is imposed by the almost quantum leap in the sums of money now involved. First Boston made a profit of $3 million in 1977; in only one quarter of 1985, it made over $44 million. Kohlberg, Kravis, Roberts and Co. reportedly will take a $45 million fee for advising itself and its partners in their proposed acquisition of Beatrice, while total fees in the transaction (financing, legal and investment advising, printing, and other expenses) have been estimated at $248 million.[55] Unless human nature has changed for the better, larger rewards seem more likely to produce more worrisome behavior.

In investment banking some conflict of interest seems guaranteed. Therefore, surely one major job of top management in investment firms is both to practice and to *preach* integrity. By "preaching," I mean continuous attempts to create and institutionalize a firm "mindset" so that it reflects the CEO's own moral and ethical convictions and values.[56] In the end, however, the individual banker remains responsible for his or her actions. We can only hope that each one recognizes the nature of the many conflicts inherent in the industry and applies (at the very least) the minimum standard recommended by a leading Wall Street lawyer: "My one and only touchstone is this. . . . I ask myself, 'How would it look in the *New York Times?*' "[57]

As for misallocation of economic resources, I fear little can be done, since it stems from fundamental human behavior. To quote Keynes one last time: "Human nature desires quick results, there is a peculiar zest in making money quickly, and remoter gains are discounted at a very high rate." Thus, a shift to genuine long-term "investing" seems as unlikely to occur as any other real change in human nature.

Today, Wall Street is a magnificent machine; it mobilizes and transfers huge sums around the world at astonishing speed. In many ways it serves society very well indeed. That it does not do a better job is not the fault of the machine, but of individuals— both those who run it and those for whose benefit it is run.

NOTES

1. James Tobin, "On the Efficiency of the Financial System," Fred Hirsch Memorial Lecture, May 15, 1984. Published in *Lloyds Bank Review* (July 1984), p. 14.

2. J. K. Galbraith, *The Great Crash* (Boston: Houghton Mifflin, 1961), p. 59.

3. Vincent P. Carosso, *Investment Banking in America* (Cambridge, Mass.: Harvard University Press, 1970), p. 285.

4. Ibid., p. 320.

5. Ibid., pp. 270, 329.

6. Quoted in T. K. McCraw, *Prophets of Regulation* (Cambridge, Mass.: Harvard University Press, 1984), p. 166. This is an excellent summary of the genesis of security regulation.

7. Carosso, op. cit., p. 257.

8. Ibid., pp. 286–87.

9. *The Proper Economic Role of the State.* Selected Papers, no. 7 (Chicago: University of Chicago, Graduate School of Business, 1963).

10. Exceptions are Susan M. Phillips and J. R. Zecher, *The SEC and the Public Interest* (Cambridge, Mass.: MIT Press, 1981), and Homer Kripke, *The SEC and Corporate Disclosure: Regulation in Search of a Purpose* (New York: Law and Business Inc., 1979).

11. See Claire Makin, "Wall Street's Electronic Cops," *Institutional Investor*, February 1986, p. 69, and Andrew Marton, "The War Against Broker Fraud," *Institutional Investor*, June 1986, pp. 109–14. The computer has also strengthened the surveillance of specialists, making possible constant NYSE monitoring of price continuity and market depth. Since specialists are often required to act against their own self-interest, the need for close monitoring seems obvious. We do not know much about their activities on regional exchanges, where the specialist may be a member of a firm that also does a public brokerage business.

12. Quoted in Martin Mayer, "Broker-Dealer Firms," in *Abuse on Wall Street*, Twentieth Century Fund (Westport, CT: Quorum Books, 1980), p. 482.

13. Irwin Friend, *Investment Banking and the New Issues Market: Summary Volume* (Philadelphia: University of Pennsylvania Press, 1965), p. 83.

14. G. J. Stigler, *The Tactics of Economic Reform*, Selected Papers, no. 13 (Chicago: University of Chicago, Graduate School of Business, 1964), p. 8. Fortunately the portfolios were hypothetical, for the investor would have lost 20 percent after one year in both periods.

15. For a review of the evidence, see Phillips and Zecher, op. cit., pp. 33–36.

16. SEC, *Institutional Investor Study Report*, 92nd Cong., 1st sess., March 10, 1971, H. Doc. 92–64, vol. 4, pp. 1596–97.

17. Mayer, op. cit., p. 461.

18. *Feit v. Leasco Data Processing Equipment Corp.*, 332 R. Supp. 544, 565 (E.D.N.Y. 1971).

19. "The Furor Over Shelf Registration," *Institutional Investor*, June 1982, p. 62.

20. J. Auerbach and S. L. Hayes, III, *Investment Banking and Diligence* (Boston: Harvard Business School Press, 1986). This is the best treatment of the issue.

21. Remarks delivered at a program of the ABA Annual Meeting, on "The Changing Environment for Financial Services and Products." Reported in *Business Lawyer*, vol. 38 (February 1983), p. 679.

22. McCraw, op. cit., p. 172.

23. Phillips and Zecher, op. cit., p. 51.

24. George J. Benston, "Required Disclosure and the Stock Market: An Evaluation of the Securities and Exchange Act of 1934," *American Economic Review* (March 1973), p. 153.

25. This may represent the tip of the iceberg. In 1984 the NYSE referred fifty suspected cases to the SEC, but only thirteen were prosecuted. See Makin, op. cit., p. 71.

26. *Business Week*, November 5, 1979, p. 87.

27. *The Wall Street Journal*, May 1, 1986, p. 1, and *Business Week*, July 14, 1986, p. 25.

28. Tobin, op. cit., p. 10.

29. A cynic might note that the Bible (Matt. 6:24) refers to God and Mammon, while the conflicts discussed below merely involve the latter.

30. Gary Slutsker, "Have We Got a Deal for You," *Forbes*, September 9, 1985, p. 34.

31. Louis Lowenstein, "Management Buyouts," *Columbia Law Review*, vol. 85, no. 4 (May 1985), p. 777.

32. Northwest's directors agreed that Northwest would indemnify the investment bank and themselves against liability in the proposed transaction. *The Wall Street Journal*, September 16, 1983, p. 12 and September 23, 1983, p. 22.

33. See William L. Silber, "Towards a Theory of Financial Innovation," in *Financial Innovation*, ed. W. L. Silber (Lexington, Mass.: Lexington Books, 1975).

34. Beth Selby, "Raiding Wars," *Institutional Investor*, February 1986, pp. 213–14.

35. J. M. Keynes, *The General Theory of Employment, Interest and Money* (New York: Harcourt, Brace, 1936); this quotation from Keynes and all subsequent ones are from chapter 12.

36. All references in this paragraph (along with references to other studies) are cited in Andrei Shleifer, "The Efficient Markets Hypothesis and the Economic Evidence of Hostile Takeovers: A Survey of Theory and Evidence." Unpublished. National Bureau of Economic Research (Washington, D.C., 1986). See also W. F. M. DeBondt and R. Thaler, "Does the Stock Market Overreact?", *Journal of Finance* (July 1985), pp. 793–807, and Lawrence H. Summers, "Do We Really Know That Financial Markets are Efficient?" *Journal of Finance* (July 1986), pp. 591–602.

37. For a discussion of this and other kinds of program trading, see chapter four of this book by Professors Light and Perold.

38. G. P. Wyser-Pratte, *Risk Arbitrage II*, New York University, Graduate School of Business Monograph (New York, 1982), p. 7.

39. See, for example, Henry G. Manne, *Insider Trading and the Stock Market* (New York: Free Press, 1966), and Matthew Farley, "A Current Look at the Law of Insider Trading," *Business Lawyer*, vol. 39, no. 4 (August 1984).

40. See page 196 of the *Report*, which devotes almost 10 percent of its space to discussion of "the market for corporate control."

41. See Michael C. Jensen, "Takeovers: Folklore and Science," *Harvard Business Review* (November–December 1984), pp. 109–21.

42. See W. A. Law, "Management Versus the Wild Bunch," *Across the Board* (June 1985), and "A Corporation Is More Than Its Stock," *Harvard Business Review* (May–June 1986), pp. 80–83.

43. *A Random Walk Down Wall Street* (New York: W. W. Norton, 1981), p. 92. Malkiel is a former security analyst and a director of a group of investment companies.

44. "It Seems Wall Street Hath No Fury Like An Adviser Scorned," *The Wall Street Journal*, May 8, 1980.

45. "A Discussion of Mergers and Acquisitions," *Midland Corporate Finance Journal*, vol. 1, no. 2 (Summer 1983), p. 27.

46. Ibid., p. 42.

47. Quoted in Geoffrey Gevalt, "In Fast Company," *Harvard Business School Bulletin* (December 1985), p. 59.

48. *Business Week*, September 30, 1985, p. 52.

49. "The Deal Makers," *The Wall Street Journal*, April 2, 1986, p. 1.

50. Ibid., and Richard Phalon, "Fuel for the Flames," *Forbes*, November 18, 1985, p. 122.

51. George D. Gibson and T. J. Campbell, "Fundamental Law for Takeovers," *Business Lawyer* (August 1984), p. 1555.

52. "The Theory of Error in Centrally Directed Economic Systems," *Quarterly Journal of Economics* (August 1964), pp. 396–419.

53. *Business Week*, November 5, 1979, p. 87.

54. Gevalt, op. cit.

55. *The Wall Street Journal*, March 19, 1986.

56. See Kenneth E. Goodpaster, "Adding Value to Value Added: The Moral Agenda of Corporate Leadership." Working Paper 9-786-003 (Boston: Harvard Business School, Division of Research, 1985). See also "Managing Greed and Risk on Wall Street," *The Economist*, July 5, 1986, p. 69.

57. Richard H. Paul, "Conflicts of Interest and the Regulation of Securities," *Business Lawyer* (January 1983), p. 568.

SEVEN

CONCLUSIONS

Samuel L. Hayes, III

With a particular focus on securities-related activities, this book has chronicled some important dimensions of the historical evolution of the U.S. financial services sector. It should be clear that the evolution of the U.S. financial framework has been importantly influenced by European banking practices and traditions as well as by domestic political philosophy and the locus of political decision making.

The American political system has always feared concentration of financial power in the hands of a few dominant institutions. It has, therefore, enacted an assortment of state and federal regulations to maintain a largely fragmented banking system. As a consequence, among world financial systems the U.S. financial services sector is unique in its size, diversity of products, and range of institutions; in 1970 there were some 50,000 financial institutions with sharply defined scopes of permitted activity in the United States.

There also has been a persistent, special political concern for the welfare of the smaller saver-investor in the financial marketplace. Recently, in addition to this populist philosophy, there has been a strong political preoccupation with the markets' operating efficiency and effectiveness in channeling funds to the most productive employment sectors. These concerns have been variously claimed by politicians and analysts as matters of "the public interest."

Although the U.S. financing sector has been given relatively free operating rein during much of the country's history, well-publicized failures and abuses have periodically surfaced and led to the perception that if the financial markets were out of control, public pressure would subsequently foster corrective legislation. The objective of each reform initiative was to deal with excesses in the financial markets, restore public confidence, and reaffirm the basic tenets of diversity in the financing industry's structure and fairness for the individual participants. As the overview of financial markets regulation in chapter two pointed out, regulation in the United States has served as the political

185

solution to the failure by markets and institutions to serve the public interest.

THE REFORMS OF THE 1930s

Investigations into the causes of the financial panic of 1929, and the onset of economic depression, uncovered numerous examples of insider abuse and intolerable conflicts of interest that were perceived to have seriously injured the public interest. The pattern of events that precipitated the regulatory reforms of the 1930s had happened before, but perhaps because of the enormity of the economic collapse and of the hardships unleashed by the Great Depression, the scope of the reforms of the 1930s was unprecedented. These new regulatory bulwarks within the U.S. financial services sector were not replicated in any other major country. To police these bulwarks, government and self-regulatory agencies were created, and for the first time, they involved themselves directly in some key day-to-day activities of financial intermediaries.

The political imperative behind this reform legislation sought (not surprisingly) to maintain and even increase the traditional fragmentation and geographic decentralization of financial services in the United States. The only exception was the securities-issuance sector, where decentralization was deemed impractical because of the physical concentration of the securities markets in New York City. The combination of this geographic reality and the regulatory thrust of the Glass-Steagall Act of 1933, which separated securities-related activities from lending and deposit-taking activities, had the practical effect of creating a distinct new genre of financial market participant: the nationwide investment bank. There was no precise historical precedent for the creation of such an institution (either in the United States or abroad) largely because there had been no perceived need to separate a bank's securities activities from its deposit and loan activities.

There is, in fact, some evidence that the framers of the Glass-Steagall Act and other reform legislation never intended to make such a complete separation of the two activities. In 1936,

Senator Carter Glass introduced amending legislation that would have permitted commercial banks to reenter the corporate securities underwriting area, but the mood in Congress was against any modifications of the 1933 reform package, and the effort failed.

The legislative changes in banking services introduced in the 1930s are having, fifty years later, a major impact on the nature of competition in the financial services sector in both the domestic and the international marketplaces. By promoting stability—in large part, by limiting the options available to savers and capital users—the legislation fostered long-term relationships between banking intermediaries and their clients and customers. This relationship banking phenomenon, discussed in the analysis of price banking in chapter three and in the analysis of shelf registrations in chapter five, already had a long history in Europe and was also evident in the pre–reform era of J. P. Morgan, Jacob Schiff, and George Baker in the United States. The newly reconstituted commercial and investment banks inherited corporate clients from their universal bank parents, and with the aid of the regulatory constraints of the 1930s, they remained linked with many of those companies (and other, newly emerging ones) in the years after World War II. Consequently, for an extended period, competition among banking intermediaries for corporate business was muted at best.

By the same token, individual savers also had limited depository alternatives and therefore tended to stay with the same institution for years. This was a major support not only to the country's commercial banks, but also to thrift institutions which, under the reform legislation, were granted a special role to collect savings deposits and to channel them, in the form of low-cost, long-term mortgages for individual home buyers, to the U.S. housing sector.

This book argues that, in effect, the regulatory agencies created to administer the reforms introduced further inefficiencies into the U.S. financing system and produced additional distortions in the allocation of financial resources within our economy. Once those regulatory bureaucracies were in place, inflexibility was inevitable. Over time, it became increasingly difficult to effect change that could respond in a timely way to alterations in the marketplace itself.

POSTWAR OPERATIONS

All the major groups of financial institutions in the United States prospered for a considerable time in the postwar period, nurtured as they were by an environment of pent-up demand, rapid economic growth, low inflation, and a stable international situation.

The securities firms were admirably positioned to exploit both the public and private financing opportunities that became available. Through their tight control of securities distribution within the protected enclave created by the Glass-Steagall Act, a group of dominant securities firms emerged. Questions did arise over whether there was sufficiently vigorous price competition among these firms, but no legislative action was taken; when the federal government initiated antitrust action against seventeen investment banks shortly after the war, the case was ultimately dismissed.

In commercial banking, regulation was perhaps most pervasive, and growth, profitability, and industry structure remained amazingly stable for nearly forty years. It was during this period that money center banks attained the status of de facto national wholesale banking institutions, although regulations limited their ability to expand physically across most state lines and, within many states, even to open additional branches. Thrift institutions also prospered in the post–World War II building boom, and insurance companies, even as they were steadily losing market share as financial intermediaries, continued to grow impressively. Each group of institutions thus managed to maintain forward momentum in those sectors that they had elected to serve or to which they had been assigned, explicitly or implicitly, by the reform legislation of the 1930s. Stable financial markets and a minimum number of banking failures seemed to be the major consequences of this system.

A change in economic conditions was in the making, however, which would ultimately put pressure on this system of regulatory-determined, segmented market niches. Beginning in the mid-1960s, a slowdown in the rate of economic growth and an acceleration in inflation had a particularly unfavorable impact on many of these established U.S. financial intermediaries. Individuals and institutions altered their savings patterns, thus changing the business mix and revenue streams of many financial institutions. At the same time, the cost structures of those organizations were also put under unusual strain. In an effort to restore satisfactory profitability, a number of firms were forced to look outside their traditional market niches for more promising opportunities.

Simultaneously, the institutionalization of savings was changing both the way in which the financial intermediaries were used and the mix of services demanded of them; the increasingly sophisticated institutional savers discussed in chapter four's treatment of institutionalization's impact on investment decision making, as well as the increasingly professional group of capital users discussed in chapter five's shelf registration analysis, were now applying elaborate quantitative analytical techniques to identify optimal financing strategies.

An enormous increase in the volume of secondary debt and equity securities transactions was yielding much greater market liquidity as well as an increased flow of investment information to more financially astute savers and capital users. Those who argued that the securities markets were now much more efficient pointed to the contemporary adeptness of financial intermediaries in their roles both as vendors of information and market exploiters of that information. They pointed to the fact, moreover, that these vendors were now servicing a much more sophisticated constituency of institutional investors and capital users. Chapter four's discussion of program trading and other portfolio optimization techniques speaks to that point; it also describes how secondary-market traders, with specific transaction objectives, subtly transmit information regarding their intentions to equally sophisticated and market-sensitive participants on the other sides of their trades. As the cost of capital rose in response to higher inflation, and as rates became more volatile as a result of the Federal Reserve's shift in monetary control in the late 1970s, both savers and capital users sought financial arrangements more finely tailored to their own special requirements; this greatly accelerated the rate of financial innovation. The rapid advances in the securitization of assets and liabilities were a part of this process of seeking more finely tuned financial arrangements between buyers and sellers of money. Under the pressure of accelerated innovation, the role of relationship banking as a support to financial intermediaries began to decline.

Although the decline of relationships hurt the position of the investment banks, chapter three makes it clear that it hurt the leading U.S. commercial banks even more. Back in the 1930s, the commercial banks had emerged from the Glass-Steagall Act's breakup of financial institutions as much the bigger and stronger of the two types of surviving entities. In the years following, however, the relative strength of the commercial banks' position had been diminished, partly as a consequence of the securitization phenomenon mentioned above. Their traditional market in short-term lines of credit for high-quality industrial borrowers was largely preempted by the growth of the commercial paper market; and an important part of their lucrative term-loan business, aimed at medium-sized and lower-rated corporate borrowers, was lost to the rapidly growing junk bond market. Further, their historically reliable and relatively low-cost deposit base was dwindling, and this compelled the banks to increasingly rely on more expensive and volatile purchased money.

The commercial banks were also affected in both the short- and the intermediate-to-long-term financing sectors by the impressive growth of the offshore financing markets. As chapter three notes, persistent U.S. balance-of-payments deficits created a growing supply of U.S. dollars held by foreigners and fostered a freewheeling, unregulated international marketplace for their employment. As this supranational market further developed, it became imperative that the United States and its financial intermediaries respond to the growing threat to the domestic financing business from this offshore capital marketplace. We have documented, for instance, how U.S. regulatory authorities, reacting to U.S. borrowers' increasing reliance on the Euromarkets for funds, ultimately freed certificates of deposit from the constraints of Regulation Q. In our treatment of shelf registrations, we have also pointed out that the SEC was compelled to move in this area in part to counteract the advantages of greater speed and flexibility available to those U.S. issuers who utilized Eurobond offerings.

MOVES TO DEREGULATE

By the early 1970s, a growing body of academic and business opinion was coming to the conclusion that regulation—whether in financial services or in other key U.S. industries—was not producing the benefits that had been historically expected of it. The U.S. political system had proven to be generally slow and cumbersome in responding to change, particularly in the regulation of financial services. Regulatory changes, when they did occur, had been largely de facto responses to particular, aggravated needs, and even then they were usually handled by administrative or rule-making powers rather than through legislative action. Many analysts believed that the entire regulatory superstructure ought to be dismantled so as to allow market forces to allocate financing resources among competing uses. As discussed throughout this book, a variety of steps, which were initiated in the 1970s, began to dismantle the regulatory superstructure governing the financial services sector.

The response of different financial intermediary groups to these new winds of competition reflected each group's particular historical circumstances. The fifty-year-old regulatory umbrella had created species of U.S. intermediaries specially adapted to the unique environment created by the reform initiatives of the 1930s, and this hothouse, self-contained environment was, in turn, maintained for many years by the preeminent global economic and financial role enjoyed by the United States in the post–World War II period. As U.S. economic hegemony declined, the hothouse environment was invaded by new and disquieting domestic and offshore financial forces that were outside the control of the system. It was in this context that effective deregulation began to be implemented, and its impact was different for several of the most important of the financial institutions that for so many years had been nurtured and controlled by the regulatory environment.

The thrift institutions, which had profitably ridden the postwar wave of home building with favorable access to fixed-rate, low-cost deposit sources, found the going particularly rough as funding sources on the right-hand side of the balance sheet became increasingly expensive and unstable, and the asset side of the balance sheet became burdened with large investments in fixed-rate, low-yielding, long-term mortgages. Although Congress considerably expanded the scope of their business franchise in the early 1980s, many of the thrifts had not developed the skills, experience, or the operating culture that were needed to make the radical departure from their regulatory-determined business focus. Similarly, retail securities brokerage firms found it difficult to adapt to the sharp competition from new entrants into their traditional product niches, especially since they were attempting at the same time to broaden their own business penetration into unfamiliar areas previously the exclusive preserve of commercial banks, thrifts, and insurance companies.

We have also chronicled how the commercial banks, originally the dominant survivors of the Glass-Steagall Act partitioning, saw their traditional product lines and service niches eroded by market developments. Many of the larger banks concluded that they must move into new product and market niches that, although conventionally identified with investment banking, offered greater profit and volume potential. Yet their resources and cultural mind-sets were also conditioned by a half-century of regulatory constraint. While many of the money-center banks made a determined effort to effect the transformation, they experienced great difficulty in adapting to the new competitive realities after so many years of regulatory-directed compartmentalization.

Ironically, it was the wholesale investment banks, primarily serving corporations and institutional investors, that appeared to be best positioned to compete in the evolving, deregulated marketplace. Although they were considered to be the runt of the litter when the big universal banks were split up in the 1930s, they benefited enormously from their exclusive franchise to undertake all corporate securities-related financing activity within the rapidly growing postwar U.S. economy. Because regulations prohibited them from commercial banking activities, they directed their natural entrepreneurial energies toward the further development of business opportunities within their sphere of permitted activities. Among other things, their initiatives created vastly more liquid markets for equity and debt instruments as well as impressive advances in financial engineering and implementation in connection with mergers and acquisitions.

THE FUTURE TRAJECTORY

Despite the upheavals, dislocations, and alterations in relative competitive position that have been caused by the process of deregulation, we do not propose its arrest or reversal. It is our conviction that it is still preferable to reregulation. We do not think that the record of the past fifty years vindicates the proposition that an extensive bureaucracy (which is inevitably influenced by short-term political imperatives) can be relied on to do a better job than a free and open market in channeling the activities of financial intermediaries and, ultimately, the flow of capital resources.

Furthermore, rapid technological change, market restructuring, and global competition are an economic reality and since all promote less-fettered capital markets, an effort by the United States to reverse course would not likely be followed by offshore markets (in contrast to what might have been the case several decades ago). As the world's money and capital markets become more and more integrated through constant arbitrage—in which a number of U.S. firms are major players—it is likely that reregulatory action would not only be counterproductive for U.S. markets, but would also fail to achieve its long-range objectives. Thus, it seems clear to us that reregulation would cost the United States and its financial institutions important global influence.

Our conviction that relatively unfettered financial markets will best serve the nation does not lead us, however, to advocate a completely laissez-faire government regulatory stance in the United States. In the broadest sense, the capital markets are simply too important to the well-being of the country to be treated with benign neglect. In order to forge the political consensus that will permit deregulation to proceed, there must be a conviction that the public interest is, in fact, being served. Earlier we identified at least three important supports for such a conviction: maintenance of competitor diversity, orderly and efficient operations of the markets themselves, and protection for the small investor-saver.

On the first count, we note that the U.S. financial markets are still highly fragmented and thus do not pose the near-term threat of undue consolidation of financial power in too few hands. Furthermore, the growing linkages between U.S. and offshore capital markets introduce a number of foreign competitors into various U.S. market sectors, and they add assurance that competition in those arenas will remain vigorous. Finally, the U.S. government's antitrust statutes provide still another stand-by protection against undue market concentration.

The second area of legitimate public policy preoccupation relates to the maintenance of continuity and orderly functioning of the markets. We are not persuaded that the purported achievement of market efficiency should be relied upon as the final arbiter of financial market direction and behavior. While we recognize that the markets have indeed made great strides in both enhanced liquidity and improved information dissemination, much data suggest that there is still a considerable distance to go before important sectors of those markets become truly efficient. In the meantime, statutes that relate to such matters as due diligence investigations to ensure the publication of all relevant issuer information must be enforced in the manner intended by their legislative framers.

There are other questions that surround the issue of market operations, such as the link between the very process of arbitraging market imperfections to achieve greater pricing efficiency and the perception that this increases short-run market volatility. As chapter four discussed, one of the consequences of the institutionalization of the markets has been a demand by portfolio managers for greater liquidity in assembling and arbitraging baskets of securities both in the cash markets and in the more recently established futures markets. These professionals shift back and forth between markets in search of price discrepancies (inefficiencies) that can be profitably exploited. Chapter four's description of program trading, by which such price discrepancies are exploited and ultimately eliminated, suggests that such short-term price lurches may be an unavoidable cost of an unbridled, self-correcting market. Moreover, it was pointed out that in this area of arbitrage activity the largest and the best-capitalized brokers enjoy a significant competitive advantage. There are, it turns out, clear economies of scale that could precipitate a further round of consolidations among firms competing in this sector of the market.

For the institutional investors, and for the securities firms that act in their behalf, there is likely to be a positive benefit in this development. And because they are in constant and close touch with each of these markets, professional players are usually able to protect themselves from the worst consequences of any price volatility that might occur. But while the portfolio managers who operate close to the center of the secondary markets have become more powerful, the more peripheral individual investors, unlikely to take advantage of the hedging and arbitrage techniques of the professionals, become weaker. This is troublesome, for we have already noted the wide-spread concern in the United States for the welfare of the individual saver-investors in the financial marketplace. Unfortunately, however, there are few (if any) regulatory responses that are likely to reduce the advantages of professional investors; these market changes that empower the professionals are the logical by-product of a long-term institutional evolution that cannot easily be reversed.

The discussion of the treatment of insider information in chapter six offers yet another caution with respect to the efficacy of a system of minimal regulatory oversight. Those who would rely on the discipline of an efficient market argue that an overall benefit accrues to the system even when a few inside information peddlers are allowed to enrich themselves by exploiting that information in personal securities transactions. It is argued that the ultimate consequence of what are, at the very least, breaches of fairness is the introduction of new information into the public domain; this then causes market prices to adjust so as to reflect the new intelligence. In a marketplace populated almost exclusively by large, sophisticated players (and this is a fair characterization of the present-day market, which is dominated by institutional investors and large corporate issuers), the short-term consequences of insider trading might, as in the case of program trading, be tolerable.

Large market participants can look after themselves. Small investors, on the other hand, are ill-equipped to fend for themselves. To the extent that such abuses continue, they do more than violate the law of the land. They jeopardize the fragile compact that has permitted the financial markets the relative freedom to innovate and experiment in recent years.

The markets of the 1980s, while immensely more liquid and sophisticated than prior to the regulations of the 1930s, are nonetheless still affected by the same sort of short-term speculation that Lord Keynes observed in the 1920s. Regulatory oversight to mitigate abuse in this competitive arena is still in the national interest. But competition itself should not be construed as the problem. Fundamentally, this competition is what creates the long-term growth and innovation that government should foster and nurture . . . albeit with care.

Contributors

JOSEPH AUERBACH holds the Class of 1957 Professor of Business Administration chair at the Harvard Business School. He earned an A.B. from Harvard College (1938) and LL.B from Harvard Law School (1941). After assignments with the Securities and Exchange Commission and the Combined Steel Group of the Allied High Commission for Germany, he joined the Boston law firm of Sullivan & Worcester, where he rose to senior partner; he now serves as counsel to the firm. His corporate practice specialized in reorganizations, railroads, pipelines, securities and administrative law matters. At the Harvard Business School, he teaches the second year M.B.A. course Law and the Corporate Manager as well as other electives. He is co-author of *Investment Banking and Diligence: What Price Deregulation?* (1986).

SAMUEL L. HAYES, III, is the Jacob H. Schiff Professor of Investment Banking at the Harvard Business School. He currently teaches the second year M.B.A. course Management of Financial Service Organizations. His research has focused on various managerial and competitive aspects of the capital markets; he has written numerous articles for the *Harvard Business Review* and other journals. He is the co-author of two previous books: *Competition in the Investment Banking Industry* (1983) and *Investment Banking and Diligence: What Price Deregulation?* (1986). Professor Hayes earned his B.A. at Swarthmore College (1957) and his M.B.A. (1961) and D.B.A. (1966) from the Harvard Business School.

WARREN A. LAW is the Edmund Cogswell Converse Professor of Finance and Banking at the Harvard Business School. He earned a B.A. (1943) at Southern Methodist University, an M.B.A. at Harvard (1948), and an M.A. and Ph.D. from Harvard (1953). Prior to joining Harvard, he served for a period as economist for the First National Bank of Dallas. At Harvard he has taught the Investment Banking course for a number of years and has written numerous papers and articles dealing with various aspects of the U.S. capital markets.

JAY O. LIGHT is professor of business administration and Chairman of the Finance Area at the Harvard Business School. He received a Bachelor of Engineering Physics from Cornell University (1964) and a D.B.A. from Harvard in 1970. After stints in the U.S. space program, in investment research, and in management consulting, he joined the Harvard faculty in 1970; he received the Salgo award for excellence in teaching in 1972. His teaching responsibilities currently focus on the second year M.B.A. courses Investment Management and Capital Markets. He is co-author of the book, *The Financial System*, and author of numerous articles and papers.

DAVID M. MEERSCHWAM is an assistant professor at the Harvard Business School. He obtained his B.S. from the London School of Economics and Political Science, and his M.A. (1981) and Ph.D. (1983) in economics from Princeton University. His main interest is international finance, especially exchange rate theory. Currently his research is concerned with international capital markets and the effects of international financial integration. Mr. Meerschwam has taught in the General Management Area of the Harvard Business School since 1983.

ANDRE F. PEROLD is an associate professor at the Harvard Business School. He received a B.Sc. (Hons) degree in mathematics and statistics from the University of the Witwatersrand (1975), and an M.S. in statistics and a Ph.D. in operations research from Stanford University (1978). Before coming to Harvard, he was awarded a post-doctoral fellowship at IBM's Thomas L. Watson Research Center in New York. He is currently teaching the second year M.B.A. course in Investment Management and his research interests cover the general area of investment management.

RICHARD H. K. VIETOR is a professor at the Harvard Business School, where he teaches courses on the regulation of business and the international political economy. His research, which focuses on business-government relations, has been published in numerous journals, and he is the author of three books: *Environmental Politics and the Coal Coalition* (1980), *Energy Policy in America Since 1945* (1984), and *Telecommunications in Transition* (1986). Mr. Vietor earned his B.A. from Union College, M.A. in history from Hofstra (1971), and Ph.D. in history from the University of Pittsburgh (1975). He taught at the University of Missouri before coming to Harvard in 1978.

INDEX